'Neil Shearing's *The Fractured Age* is a superb account of China's challenge to American dominance of the global economy.'

Praise for The Fractured Age

'An exceptionally sensible, clear-headed and original thinker.'

Martin Wolf CBE, *The Financial Times*

'Neil Shearing has written a very timely book on the new, fractured world we find ourselves in, and how governments, businesses and investors should respond.'

David Smith, Economics Editor,
The Sunday Times

'Neil Shearing is one of the most accomplished macro-economists of his generation.

Roger Bootle, author, *THE AI ECONOMY*
and former Group Chief Economist,
HSBC Banking Group

'*The Fractured Age* is a masterpiece. The best book on the future of the global economy on the market today.'

David Smick, NEW YORK TIMES
bestselling author, founder and Editor,
THE INTERNATIONAL ECONOMY magazine

'In this timely and clearly-written book, Neil Shearing lays bare the longer-term geopolitical forces at work behind the fracturing of the global trading system. He makes a compelling case that the clash between the US and China predated Donald Trump's arrival in the White House, and will persist long after he has gone.'

Heather Stewart, Economics Editor,
The Guardian

The Fractured Age

*How the Return of Geopolitics Will Splinter
the Global Economy*

Neil Shearing

JOHN
MURRAY
BUSINESS

First published by John Murray Business in 2025
An imprint of John Murray Press

1

A CIP catalogue record for this title is available from the British Library

Hardback ISBN 9781399825726
Trade Paperback ISBN 9781399825733
ebook ISBN 9781399825740

Typeset by KnowledgeWorks Global Ltd.

Printed and bound in Great Britain by Clays Ltd, Elcograf S.p.A.

John Murray Press policy is to use papers that are natural, renewable
and recyclable products and made from wood grown in sustainable
forests. The logging and manufacturing processes are expected to
conform to the environmental regulations of the country of origin.

John Murray Press
Carmelite House
50 Victoria Embankment
London EC4Y 0DZ

John Murray Business
123 S. Broad St., Ste 2750
Philadelphia, PA 19109

https://johnmurraybusiness.com/

John Murray Press, part of Hodder & Stoughton Limited

An Hachette UK company

The authorised representative in the EEA is Hachette Ireland,
8 Castlecourt Centre, Dublin 15, D15 XTP3, Ireland (email: info@hbgi.ie)

For Nicky, Evie and Josh

Contents

Preface

Globalization, once heralded as the unstoppable tide shaping our world, now stands on uncertain ground. The re-election of President Donald Trump in November 2024, won on the back of promises to impose sweeping tariffs on America's trading partners, reignited fears that the globalized world order is crumbling. Yet, despite nearly a decade of protectionist measures – first initiated by Trump and sustained, even expanded, under President Biden – global trade remains near record highs. Trump's return to office raised the stakes, stoking fears of an impending trade war that could devastate the world economy. But for now, the heated rhetoric of Trump and other populist leaders has yet to cause a collapse in the flow of goods and services around the globe.

This book argues that an alternative way to view the changes that are being wrought upon the global economy is through the lens of superpower rivalry. The globalization era has ended but the world isn't necessarily deglobalizing. Instead, the US and China are pulling apart and, as they do so, other countries are coming under pressure to pick sides. The fault lines along which this fracturing takes place will define our collective economic prospects over the next decade. This is the subject of this book.

The first chapter provides an overview of the key arguments and conclusions. It acts as a form of executive summary. Subsequent chapters explore the drivers of fracturing, how different countries might align in a fractured world and the potential consequences for, among other things, world trade, global supply chains, international investment, cross-border transfers of technology and the race to secure supplies of critical minerals. The final chapter sketches out what the global economy might look like a decade from now.

This book is not intended to be the final word on this subject – not least because fracturing is a process that is in flux. But it is intended as a framework for thinking about the forces that will shape the global economy over the coming decade. In doing so, I hope that it allows corporate leaders to make better-informed decisions about their businesses – and helps prevent governments on both sides of the divide from getting sucked into more extreme forms of fracturing that would have dire consequences for us all.

Prologue

Ren Zhengfei is no ordinary communist. Born in 1944 in Guizhou, a mountainous province in southwest China, his family was one of relatively modest means. His father started university but dropped out before graduating following the death of Ren's grandfather. Ren's childhood was marked by huge political and economic turmoil in China. The Chinese Communist Party's victory against the Nationalists in 1949 swept Mao Zedong to power, bringing wrenching economic and societal change. In 1958, Mao initiated the Great Leap Forward – a bold yet disastrous attempt to transform China from an agrarian society to a modern industrialized economy. Grinding poverty and widespread famine ensued. Millions lost their lives.

Guizhou was not spared the hardships of the period and Ren's own account of his childhood tells of repeated struggles. His father became a teacher in the local school but still struggled to feed a family of nine. Despite the desperate background, Ren gained a place at Chongqing University to study engineering. Then, in 1966, came another wrenching change: Mao's Cultural Revolution.

The Cultural Revolution was neither cultural nor revolutionary. Rather, it was a concerted attempt by Mao to maintain control, eliminate dissent and enforce ideological purity. As both a teacher and a former employee in the Nationalist government, Ren's father came under immediate suspicion and was removed from his position, throwing the family into renewed turmoil.

A turning point

The turning point for Ren came in 1968, when he graduated from college and joined the Engineering Corps of the 304th Battalion of the People's Liberation Army (PLA). Details of exactly what Ren did in the PLA are hazy but we know that he won several awards for his contributions in the field of chemical engineering before developing an interest in telecoms. His attempts to join the Party were repeatedly rebuffed because of his father's links to the Nationalist government, but in 1978 he was finally admitted. This coincided with China's government embarking on a major programme of economic reform and liberalization under Deng Xiaoping. Price controls were relaxed, markets were given a greater role in allocating resources and Deng announced a new 'Open Door Policy' that would allow foreign businesses to set up in China.

As China liberalized, Ren grew disenchanted with life in the army. The PLA was the place to forge a reputation in 1970s China, but by the 1980s the action was in the private sector. In 1982, faced with the prospect of transferral to a scientific research base, Ren resigned from the army and made a break for the private sector. His early endeavours were not entirely successful. He bounced between jobs and achieved some success as the deputy general manager of an electronics company, before being cheated out of a sizeable amount of money by a rogue businessman.[1]

Nonetheless, Ren's experience in the PLA had given him exposure to the telecoms sector, which was undergoing rapid expansion both within China and overseas. In 1987, Ren founded his own telecoms firm, calling it Shenzhen Huawei Technology Company, or Huawei for short. There are various interpretations of the name Huawei, including 'Connected to China' and 'China is able'. Both encapsulate the spirit of the age.

Huawei initially focussed on producing phone switches for the booming domestic market. Realizing that the firm could not compete with cheaper products from overseas, Ren decided to import component parts and then assemble them in China – while at the same time employing a team of engineers to develop domestically-produced alternatives to the imported components.

The results were spectacular. Huawei's growth was explosive and the firm swiftly expanded into the broader telecoms market. Its cheap but high-quality products gained traction worldwide, enabling the company to secure partnerships with several international telecom operators. Huawei's first contract outside China and Hong Kong came in 1997, when it secured an agreement with Telekom Malaysia to expand and improve telecoms infrastructure in Malaysia. This provided a launchpad for expanding Huawei's footprint beyond China.

Globalization's promise

However, the watershed moment for Ren and for Huawei came in 2001, with China's accession to the World Trade Organization (WTO). Trade tariffs had been falling globally for several years as Western economies liberalized and emerging economies opened up. According to World Bank data, the global average tariff rate fell from 8.6 per cent in 1994 to 5 per cent in 2000. For those pushing for global integration, the entry of China – and its market of 1.3 billion people – into the world trading system held the key to turbo-charging globalization. By 2006 average tariffs had fallen to little more than 3 per cent.[2]

WTO accession meant that Huawei could now source component parts from and ship final goods to international markets without incurring punitive tariffs. This accelerated its expansion into new areas, including consumer electronics. But the legal protections afforded by the WTO also provided a springboard for Huawei's international expansion in core areas of telecoms infrastructure. In 2005, the firm signed an agreement with IBM to develop 'BladeCenter' servers, a collaboration which combined IBM's server technology with Huawei's telecoms expertise. In the same year, Huawei entered into partnership with BT Telecom to upgrade the UK's telecoms infrastructure. Partnerships across the US, Canada, Europe and Asia followed.

In less than 20 years Huawei went from a scrappy start-up to a global leader. By 2012 it had become the largest telecoms equipment manufacturer in the world. By 2016, 9 per cent of all mobile phones sold worldwide were produced by Huawei, increasing to 16 per cent by 2019.³ In the same year, the firm logged global revenues of around $122bn, putting it on par with Microsoft.⁴

Huawei's spectacular growth could not have been possible without the integration of global supply chains and the opening up of international markets. Ren Zhengfei and the company he built came to embody the age of globalization that reshaped the world economy in the 1990s and 2000s: dynamic, outward-facing and extremely profitable.

However, while Ren became a poster child for the opportunities made possible by globalization, over time his company became a lightning rod for concerns about China's emergence as an economic and geopolitical rival to the US.

For two decades from the early-1990s, governments in all the world's major economies shared a common view that their people's wellbeing and prosperity were best served by increasing economic and financial integration with the rest of the world. The common view in the rich world, in Latin America, in fast-growing Asia and in countries emerging from the collapse of the Soviet bloc was that globalization would bring economic benefits. And in the West in particular, there was a parallel belief that globalization would help mould other parts of the world in the West's image and so foster a more stable and secure world too. New entrants to the global economy would become 'responsible stakeholders' in the Western-centred, liberal, democratically-inclined world order, as former US Deputy Secretary of State, Robert Zoellick, put it.⁵

China's challenge

However, from the mid-2010s faith in that view started to wane. This was due in part to a growing recognition that globalization brought costs as well as benefits to Western economies: decaying industrial sectors, rising inequality and a loss of social cohesion were all attributable in some part to globalization. But it was also because after the accession to power of Xi Jinping in 2012, it gradually became clear that China had no intention of liberalizing politically but every intention of harnessing global trade and technology flows to help it become a strategic rival to the US.

Huawei came under increasing scrutiny over its alleged ties to the Chinese government. In December 2018, Ren's daughter and the firm's chief financial officer, Meng Wanzhou, was arrested upon entry to Canada on allegations that Huawei had violated sanctions against Iran.[6] China responded by arresting two Canadians, Michael Spavor and Michael Kovrig, on allegations of espionage. All three were eventually released in September 2021, but growing strains between China and the West had been catapulted into public view. The direction of travel was clear.

In May 2019, the US Department of Commerce added Huawei to its 'Entity List', which restricted American companies from doing business with Huawei without government approval. The following year it tightened restrictions, requiring all semiconductor manufacturers using US technology to obtain a licence before supplying chips to Huawei. In one fell swoop, the US government removed the firm's access to the most advanced component parts. European governments were slower to react but started to follow in

America's footsteps. In 2020 the UK government announced that Huawei would not be permitted to bid on contracts to build the country's 5G telecoms network. France, Italy and Germany are also taking steps to phase out the firm from their mobile networks.

Huawei's success was built on an open and integrated global economy which provided access to technology and a large market. Now it is having to adapt to being cut off. Domestic sales in China hit a record high in the first quarter of 2024,[7] but sales outside of China remained $60bn lower than their peak in 2020.[8]

The fractured world

Many argue that the story of Huawei is of little relevance to the rest of the world. Huawei's sales in the US have slumped but China's exports to the US more generally are holding up. Meanwhile, global trade in goods and services was around $31trn in 2023, close to a record high.[9]

However, this book takes a different view. It argues that Huawei's struggles are symptomatic of how China's emergence as a strategic rival to the US is reshaping the world economy – and that the effects will be felt by all. The world will not deglobalize, but rather fracture into two blocs: one with the US at its core and another with China at its core. Policy choices within each bloc will be driven increasingly by geopolitical as well as economic considerations. However, while this will have profound implications in some areas of global trade and finance, in other areas life will continue pretty much as normal. Understanding where the fault lines sit will be crucial if policymakers, investors and corporate leaders are to successfully navigate the fracturing world.

How deeply into our everyday lives will these geopolitical forces reach? Will the US squander its strong starting point by antagonizing allies or adopting a more isolationist position under a second Trump administration? How will domestic politics in each bloc shift in the face of fracturing? Most ominously, what would happen if the two blocs came into conflict? These are the questions that will shape the world over the next decade or so – and they are the ones that this book sets out to answer.

CHAPTER 1

The Fractured Age

Globalization has woven an intricate web connecting distant corners of the world, transforming our lives in ways that are both obvious and subtle. Walk into an American electronics store and you'll find sleek Apple devices, assembled in China, sitting next to Samsung televisions, engineered in South Korea. Wander through a European shopping mall and racks of fast fashion from brands like Zara and H&M – produced in Bangladesh or Vietnam – offer the latest styles at prices unimaginable just a generation ago. Open a pension or retirement plan and you will be confronted with an array of options to invest your savings across the world.

But the story of globalization is not only about the West's access to cheaper goods and exotic investment opportunities, it is also about the transformation of lives and livelihoods in emerging markets. Over the past three decades, China has been transformed into the world's largest manufacturer and its biggest exporter – a process that has lifted hundreds of millions of people out of poverty and created entire cities. In countries like Vietnam, Bangladesh and India, the growth of export-driven industries has provided employment for millions, helping boost local economies and improve living standards. Workers, many of whom would have relied on subsistence agriculture in the past, now have access to more stable incomes, healthcare and education. This shift has fuelled a growing middle class with the purchasing power to buy the very goods they help produce, sparking a cycle of rapid economic development across emerging markets.

An immutable force?

It is tempting to think that the global economy as we have come to know it is fundamentally immune to change. Six years on from the start of Donald Trump's first trade war with China, US–China trade volumes hit a record high in 2023. Global trade of goods and services has increased by more than 40 per cent since Trump was first elected in 2016.[1] Talk of 'reshoring' production to the US and Europe remains just that – talk. And even if governments and businesses were willing to stomach the huge costs associated with 'deglobalizing', they would struggle to unravel the complex network of global supply chains that has become embedded over the past three decades.

The story of Foxconn in Wisconsin provides grist to the mill of those who believe in the enduring resilience of globalization. In 2017, the Taiwan-headquartered firm, which is the world's largest contract manufacturer of electronics and a major supplier to Apple, announced that it would build a $10bn facility in Mount Pleasant, Wisconsin, to produce large LCD screens. The move was heralded by then-President Trump as the start of a great reshoring of manufacturing jobs to America: never one for understatement, Trump called the plant the 'eighth wonder of the world'. It was intended that the plant would initially employ 3,000 workers in Wisconsin, but that this figure would eventually rise to 13,000.[2]

Yet the plant has fallen well short of lofty expectations. The $10bn investment that was initially promised by Foxconn has been reduced to just $670mn.[3] The number of jobs it is expected to create has been revised down to just 1,400. It is easy for politicians to rail against the perceived costs of globalization but the lesson from Wisconsin is that it is much harder to do something about it.

A world in flux

Globalization may not have met its match in Wisconsin, but it is less resilient than many have come to assume. In fact, the rules by which we organize the global economy change with alarming regularity, with periods of openness and integration giving way to long spells in which economies turn inwards.

The most notorious example comes from the period between the First and Second World Wars. The late nineteenth century witnessed the first modern era of globalization. Between 1870 and 1914 trade between the US and Europe flourished and immigration surged. There were also large capital flows from Europe to the US and some parts of Latin America, notably Argentina. But economic integration was brought to a halt by the First World War and then ultimately reversed by a period of 'beggar thy neighbour' protectionism that followed in the wake of the

Great Depression. Both global trade and global industrial production fell by around 30 per cent in the early 1930s.[4]

The aftermath of the Second World War also witnessed a period of economic integration between the world's major economies that then stalled in the 1970s and 1980s. This was due in part to a policy of so-called 'trade restraint' in the US under President Reagan, which attempted to push back against an influx of cheap imports from Japan and other countries in Asia. The economic fallout was very different from the 1930s, with global integration stalling rather than reversing. But the lessons from the past 150 years are clear: there is nothing inevitable about globalization, and when periods of economic integration end it is usually because of the actions of governments.

We are once again at a moment of change. China's emergence as a strategic rival to the US – and the subsequent return of geopolitics as a driver of policy decisions and economic outcomes – will consign the recent era of hyper-globalization to the archive. Yet what will follow remains highly uncertain. In order to understand what comes next, we need to understand how we arrived at the current juncture.

False promises

As the Cold War ended, the US political scientist Francis Fukuyama famously declared 'the end of history'.[5] Liberal democracy had triumphed over state communism. From an economic perspective, free market capitalism had prevailed over central planning. Policy across the globe became heavily influenced by what was called the 'Washington Consensus'.

This emphasized the central importance of the market, and it promoted openness to both trade and capital flows.

The objective in Washington was simple: to bring the emerging markets of Asia, Latin America and Eastern Europe into a US-led capitalist system.

But these economies were not just supplicants to a US plan to mould the world in its own image. They had seen first-hand the flaws of central planning in China and Eastern Europe, as well as the financial chaos of state-led capitalism in Latin America. Economic liberalization and integration with the rest of the world were viewed as a path to prosperity. Accordingly, while liberalizing reforms were sometimes given a helpful nudge by conditions attached to International Monetary Fund (IMF) programmes, in many cases they resulted from domestically-driven shifts in policy. This was most obviously the case in China, which began a programme of market-oriented reforms that started in 1978 under Deng Xiaoping and culminated in the country joining the World Trade Organization in 2001 – which, it is worth noting, is barely a generation ago.

For a time, the plan seemed to benefit everyone. China's share of world gross domestic product (GDP) soared from 3.5 per cent in 2000 to just under 15 per cent in 2015 (measured at market exchange rates). Over the same period, India's economy nearly tripled in size, Indonesia's doubled, and Poland's and Brazil's grew by 65 per cent and 50 per cent respectively. This was a golden age of emerging market growth. America's share of global GDP diminished, but it held a smaller share of a bigger pie. Between 2001 and 2008 real GDP per head in the US increased by over 10 per cent.[6] More fundamentally, the world seemed more

'American'. Emerging economies embraced market-oriented reforms, and some undertook politically liberalizing reforms. The collapse of the Soviet Union cemented the US's position as the world's sole economic and political superpower.

Yet during the past decade or so, this understanding of how the world should work has started to fall apart. It is tempting to point to Donald Trump's first election victory in 2016 as the moment when things changed. His views on economic policy seemed drawn from an earlier, pre-globalization era – multilateralism replaced by unilateral measures like tariffs to hold foreign firms and investors at bay.

But it is telling that there was no pressure for his policies to be reversed once he left office. If anything, the scope of US state intervention in the workings of global markets widened under Joe Biden, with stringent bans on technology exports to China and on access to the US financial system by Russian firms, as well as increased state support for strategically important industries such as semiconductors and electric vehicles (EVs). And this retreat from openness wasn't just happening in the US. Countries from the Netherlands to Japan either went along with US sanctions or introduced similar measures of their own.

China's challenge

In fact, the turning point predates the first Trump presidency. It occurred instead in the period between the eruption of the Global Financial Crisis in 2007–08 and the accession to the leadership in China of Xi Jinping in 2012.

Before this period it was still possible to believe that increasing global integration was helping to spread prosperity and common liberal values around the world. But the economic collapse and subsequent slow recovery from the Global Financial Crisis (GFC) focussed Western attention on the vulnerabilities and regional inequalities caused by globalization.

At the same time, Xi Jinping showed it was a mistake to believe that economic integration would foster the spread of common values. Initially, Xi was viewed by some as a leader who would deepen China's market reforms. In practice, economic and political reforms have gone backwards. The overriding priority under Xi has been to reassert the primacy of the Communist Party in domestic life and to advance China's position as a global superpower. China's government has become more repressive at home and more assertive on the world stage. Economic policy has shifted to accommodate these objectives.

The 'Made in China 2025' project, which was announced in 2015, signalled this change to the rest of the world. It made clear that Beijing intended to become self-sufficient in cutting-edge technologies, which until then had been under the monopoly of the West. At the same time, the Belt and Road Initiative (BRI), a 'new Silk Road', was developed as a vehicle for Beijing to project its power around the world. It became a conduit for billions of dollars of investment in emerging economies across Asia, Africa and Latin America, expanding China's political and economic influence in these regions in the process.

In all this, China's emergence as an economic superpower was key. The West might have been happy to coexist – and trade freely – with a politically-repressive China that was economically middling in size. But, by the early-2010s, China had overtaken the US on some measures of economic heft. It became the world's biggest goods exporter in 2009 and the largest manufacturer in 2012. A decade later, China's manufacturing sector was bigger than the next three largest, the US, Germany and Japan, combined. And China's economic resurgence was providing it with resources to expand militarily. Xi and China posed a threat to US interests that was becoming increasingly difficult for Washington to ignore.

The global economy was then hit by two shocks. First, COVID-19 struck in 2020 and forced governments and companies to reconsider the risks associated with global supply chains. And second, Russia's 2022 invasion of Ukraine thrust the issue of energy security into the open. The sanctions placed on Moscow also demonstrated how the financial and technological might of the West could be brought to bear against a rival.

Both of these shocks pitted Washington against Beijing. Collectively, they accelerated the end of the era of 'hyperglobalization' that defined the 1990s and 2000s. Governments now view integration not as a route to prosperity and shared values but also as a source of risk and instability. We have entered an era of geopolitical rivalry and geoeconomic fracturing.

A challenge to be managed rather than overcome

One important point to make clear from the outset is that fracturing is not simply globalization in reverse. The world is not necessarily 'deglobalizing'. Indeed, global trade has continued to increase and cross-border capital flows remain high by historic standards. Rather, a deepening economic and geopolitical rivalry is pitting the US and China against one another. This is causing relations between the world's two economic superpowers to fracture. As they do so, other countries will come under pressure to pick a side.

Many countries would, of course, prefer to remain neutral and some will successfully straddle the two blocs. But over time it will become increasingly difficult to do so. It is tempting to think that the re-election of Donald Trump has fatally undermined the idea of a US-bloc: the US now views *every* country merely as some form of economic adversary; it is now Washington against the world. But while Trump's re-election will strain relations between the US and its allies in Europe and Asia, it is likely that containing China will remain a key objective of US policy. If it is to meet this objective, then the US will need support from its allies.

With Trump in the White House the path ahead is exceptionally uncertain. A period of US isolationism is possible, the consequences of which I discuss in detail in Chapter 8. But viewed over a longer horizon, I believe that a more likely outcome is that in the decades ahead the world will split into a Western bloc that is broadly aligned with the US and another that is broadly aligned with China. Countries within each bloc will not always see eye-to-eye. Indeed, there will often be periods in which they disagree on issues. But they will share a similar set of values. And as the superpower rivalry between the US and China deepens, policy decisions on both sides will be shaped by geopolitical considerations. This is the essence of the fractured world.

One response to the strains that threaten today's global economic order is to try to shake the world's leaders from complacency, to remind them of the enormous gains made over the past 30 years of globalization that could be lost. But this effort misunderstands why fracturing is happening – in particular that it is something that governments on both sides of the geopolitical divide are actively pursuing. The key question therefore is not whether global fracturing can be averted, but what form it will take. From an economic perspective, two issues are critical: the likely composition of the blocs, and how deep and how wide the fracturing goes.

Mapping the fractured world

Whether countries side with the US or China will depend on the extent of their economic, financial, political and social ties. Chapter 3 discusses this in depth and maps how different countries might align in a fractured world. A key point is that boundaries between blocs are fuzzy and the strength of allegiances within them will shift over time. As is becoming clear, Donald Trump's return to the White House is causing strains with key allies in Europe. With that said, however, the broad contours of a fractured world are already starting to form. Canada, Japan, Korea and the overwhelming majority of countries in Europe remain natural – if sometimes uncomfortable – allies of the US. Meanwhile, Russia, Iran and Venezuela will sit in China's bloc, and large parts of Sub-Saharan Africa will lean towards Beijing too.

But some countries are more difficult to place. Vietnam is closely linked into Chinese supply chains, but strong diplomatic ties to Washington mean it is an important US ally in South-East Asia. Conversely, Saudi Arabia has historically been a strong US partner but growing economic and political ties to China are pushing it closer to Beijing.

India will be a key player in fracturing. It is the world's largest country by population and the fastest growing major economy. By the end of this decade it is likely to have overtaken Japan and Germany to become the world's third largest economy when measured at market exchange rates. Alongside China, India is the most important member of the BRICS group of large emerging economies. This, coupled with the authoritarian tendencies of its Prime Minister Narendra Modi, have led many to assume that India will side with China.

But the two countries are rivals as much as they are allies. They have a long-running border dispute that periodically threatens to break out into conflict. What's more, India is one of a handful of countries that could benefit from the economic dislocation caused by fracturing – though only if it can position itself as a reliable US ally. India's position in a fractured world is unclear, but it is wrong to assume it will side with China. On balance, it seems more likely to lean towards the US.

Friends matter

The size and composition of blocs is important because in a fractured world friends will matter. For one thing, a country's economic (and political) heft will be determined in part by the strength of its alliances with others. The financial sanctions that the US placed on Russia in the wake of its invasion of Ukraine were made more effective by the fact that European nations imposed similar measures.

As things stand, the population of the two blocs is shaping up to be roughly equal. But the US-bloc is far larger economically. The US and countries that are currently close allies or lean towards it account for about 70 per cent of global GDP at market exchange rates. In contrast, the China-bloc accounts for about 25 per cent of global GDP.[7] (A small number of countries will remain unaligned.)

The US-bloc is also shaping up to be more economically diverse than the China-bloc. This is important because the greater the differences within each bloc, the easier it will be to replicate the global economy at large.

America has on its side high-income knowledge economies (such as the UK), cutting-edge manufacturers (Taiwan, Korea, Japan and Germany), low-income manufacturers (Vietnam and Mexico) and major commodity producers like Canada and Australia. In contrast, China's allies fall into one of two buckets: autocracies or commodity producers (and often both).

This will give China an edge over the US in securing supplies of strategically important minerals, including those needed for the green transition. But it means that the US is likely to retain a technological advantage over China in several areas, and the greater economic diversity of its bloc will make it easier to adapt to the challenges posed by fracturing.

How deep, how wide?

This brings us to the second factor that will influence the economic consequences of fracturing, which is how deep and how wide the fissure between the two blocs becomes. This is perhaps the most important question relating to fracturing – and one of the greatest areas of uncertainty. The answer will depend on the actions, and responses to those actions, of governments on both sides over the next decade. This is inherently unknowable. Trump's re-election risks a much wider break, not just between America and China but also between America and its traditional allies. It is possible that the threat to impose stringent tariffs on China, Mexico and other US trading partners – including Europe – could tip the world into a trade war that produces a period of deglobalization similar to that experienced in the inter-war years. The economic costs could be huge.

But this is not bound to happen. For one thing, the size and scope of trade restrictions are critical. The tariffs levied during the first Trump administration (which were kept in place under Biden) had relatively little impact on global trade volumes: both exports from China and imports to the US in 2024 ran at close to record highs.

The threat of protectionism needs to be taken seriously and the economic consequences could be devastating. But when formulating a central case for how global economic relations will evolve over the next two decades it makes sense to focus on where there is broad consensus. In this respect, it is important to keep in mind that Trump can serve only one more term as president and that while there is broad support across the US political spectrum to counter the economic and geopolitical threat posed by China, support for a wider trade war is more limited. Taken together, that provides some hope that the split that both sides will ultimately pursue is a partial one focussed on areas of strategic importance.

Wind the clock forward ten years and it is likely that the US will continue to import large quantities of low-end goods from China and other emerging economies. Meanwhile, governments elsewhere in the world, from Germany to Japan, will have strong trade links to China that they will try to preserve. It is therefore likely that trade in many areas will continue with relatively modest additional costs or frictions.

However, fracturing will bring significant change to sectors that governments view as strategically important. This is likely to include areas such as semiconductors, high-capacity batteries, critical minerals, pharmaceuticals, aerospace, and cloud and edge computing. It will also include products that handle large amounts of personal data. Decisions about the location of production in these areas will be made on the basis of national security rather than economic efficiency. Multinational firms operating in these sectors are likely to find themselves subject to increased government pressure and oversight.

Efforts to secure supply chains in these areas are already being reflected in policy. The CHIPS Act, which was passed by US Congress in 2022, contained $39bn of subsidies for domestic semiconductor manufacturing over a five-year period – and a ban on recipients of that money expanding semiconductor manufacturing in China and other 'countries of concern'. In the same year, Congress also passed the Inflation Reduction Act, which raised tax credits for electric vehicle production provided that the vehicles are assembled in North America and that the battery minerals or component parts are not sourced from 'foreign entities of concern'. This includes China and Russia.

Governments in Europe are starting to follow in America's footsteps. In January 2023, the European Union (EU) announced the formation of the Green Deal Industrial Plan, one pillar of which will be to increase the resilience of supply chains in green technology. It also announced plans to launch the European Sovereignty Fund, which will provide funding to secure supplies of batteries, hydrogen, semiconductors and other critical raw materials.

Europe's plans are smaller and less developed than those of the US, but the direction of travel is clear. What's more, such policies are likely to be the thin end of a long wedge. Over time they will have a profound effect on supply chains and trade flows in areas deemed to be of strategic importance. In the future, everyday products that contain high-tech components, such as the phones we use and the cars we drive, are likely to be sourced within blocs. At the same time, however, large parts of the global trading system that are not considered to be strategically important will be unaffected. Western consumers will continue to fill their homes with goods that are made in China, from toys and games to clothes and furniture.

Fracturing ≠ deglobalization

Accordingly, while fracturing will touch all of our lives, it will not necessarily lead to a significant rollback in global trade. For one thing, trade between the US and China-blocs accounts for only 25 per cent of total world trade.[8] And only a small share of this trade is in areas that might be viewed as important from the perspective of national security. If fracturing is contained to these areas, it may affect less than 5 per cent of global trade.

What's more, if Western governments push to sever ties with China in these sectors, production is most likely to move to another low-cost producer that is more closely aligned with the US and its allies. Having manufactured iPhones in its mega-factory in Zhengzhou in central China since 2010, Apple is now producing its latest model in a new facility just outside Chennai in southern India. By 2025 the firm estimates that it will manufacture almost 50 million phones in India – equivalent to a quarter of its global production.[9] Other parts of the iPhone supply chain are likely to follow.

This shift is being replicated by other firms. In recent years, Samsung, Nike and Adidas have moved production from China to Vietnam, Dell has announced plans to move from China to Mexico and Hewlett-Packard is planning to shift some of its operations from China to Thailand. All of this will continue to involve trade.

The deepening geopolitical rivalry between the US and China will therefore present opportunities for emerging economies that can position themselves as reliable allies of Washington. This includes Mexico, Vietnam, India and Poland.

The counterpart, however, is that it is doubtful that the great 'reshoring' of manufacturing jobs to the US that has been promised by Donald Trump and others will materialize on a significant scale. Accordingly, those searching for evidence of fracturing in a fall in global trade are looking in the wrong place. Having surged in the 1990s and 2000s, trade in goods and services as a share of global GDP peaked in 2010. A reasonable base case is that it flatlines as a share of global GDP over the next decade.

Fracturing and the global financial system

US–China fracturing will also have significant ramifications for the global financial system. The wave of globalization that reshaped the world economy in the 1990s and 2000s was different from previous periods of global integration in part because it contained a large financial element. Between 1990 and 2018, there was a five-fold increase in cross-border bond and equity flows and a seven-fold increase of foreign direct investment flows. In addition to the globalization of production, the world experienced the globalization of finance.

This has created a complex web of cross-border financial claims that was not a feature of previous periods of globalization. To put this into context, the gross external assets of the US, UK, France, Germany, Netherlands, Canada and Japan peaked at about 20 per cent of their collective GDP during the first modern wave of globalization around the turn of the twentieth century. During this latest wave of globalization they rose from about 30 per cent of GDP in 1990 to over 100 per cent of GDP in 2018.[10]

At the same time, emerging economies, led by China, have become deeply integrated within the global financial system. The most obvious illustration of this is the huge increase in China's holdings of US Treasury bonds, which increased from $60bn in 2000 to over $750bn in 2023.[11] However, this actually understates the extent to which China has accumulated external assets and the degree of financial integration that has taken place between blocs. China's financial claims on the US and US-aligned countries are probably more than $5trn.[12]

The internationalization of finance has been a defining feature of the global economy over the past 30 years. It has enabled households to invest their pensions in far flung corners of the world, and it has expanded the global pool of capital from which firms and governments can borrow to finance themselves. Financial integration has also been fundamental to the rapid growth of global cities, including New York, London, Hong Kong and Singapore.

It is often argued that financial globalization – and in particular the increase in China's external assets – has tipped the balance of global financial power in Beijing's favour. In fact, the opposite is true – financial integration over the past three decades has increased the importance of the US within the global financial system. This is because the vast majority of cross-border flows are denominated in US dollars. According to the Bank for International Settlements, around 90 per cent of foreign exchange transactions in 2022 were settled in US dollars.[13] At some point, these transactions will have touched the US financial system.

The result is that the US now provides the financial plumbing for the world economy. This in turn has conveyed enormous power and influence on America. The central importance of the US to the global financial system was made clear in the periods of acute stress that followed the 2008 Global Financial Crisis and the 2020 COVID-19 pandemic, in which the Fed acted as de facto lender of last resort to the global banking system. More ominously for US adversaries, it was also reflected in the ability of Washington and its allies to impose heavy financial sanctions on Russia in the wake of its invasion of Ukraine.

Financial fracturing in action

The effect of fracturing on the global financial system will in practice depend on two things. The first is how it affects international capital flows, and the second is whether it leads to an unwinding of the cross-border investments that were created in the globalization era. The answer in both cases will depend on the form that fracturing takes. But just as fracturing will not necessarily lead to a sharp fall in world trade, only under an extreme form of fracturing is it likely that the world will become significantly less financially integrated.

A more likely outcome is that, having far outstripped the growth of global GDP over the past two decades, international capital flows now grow at a similar rate to global GDP over the coming decade. Meanwhile, unless fracturing takes an extreme form, it is unlikely that there will be a significant unwinding of aggregate cross-border investments. For a start, despite the integration of China within the global financial system, the overwhelming majority of cross-border financial flows take place between US-aligned countries. Cross-border financial claims within the US-bloc are almost ten times larger than those between the US- and China-blocs – and they are unlikely to be affected by global fracturing.[14]

There is a greater risk that fracturing leads to efforts to unwind financial claims between the US- and China-aligned blocs. But there are powerful forces acting against this. Most obviously, any push by either side to offload these assets would lead to a drop in their price. As a result, unless they were able to divest their entire stock of assets in one go then they would be hit with a financial loss on the portion that they retained.

There is also the question of where and how the proceeds would be reinvested. A recurrent concern in financial markets is that Beijing will 'dump' its holdings of US Treasuries, leading to a sharp and destabilizing rise in the cost of borrowing for the US government and, by extension, US firms. But such concerns ignore the fact that there are few markets outside the US Treasury market that are large enough to absorb a significant amount of China's enormous external assets. What's more, a key reason for Beijing to reduce its holdings of US Treasuries would be to limit its exposure to the type of punitive sanctions placed on Russia. But any alternative asset class to US Treasuries would almost certainly be denominated in dollars or a currency of a US ally, such as the euro, and therefore also liable to US or Western sanctions.

Dollar dominance is here to stay

It is for this reason that several commentators have suggested that China and its allies will seek to develop alternatives to the US dollar, both as a currency in which to transact and also one in which to invest. And as fracturing develops it is likely that over the next decade more trade and investment between China and its allies will take place in renminbi. But this is unlikely to seriously threaten the dollar's position.

For one thing, the China-bloc is likely to account for a relatively small share of the global economy. Trade within it currently represents just over 5 per cent of total world trade. China's importance to the global economy has increased substantially over the past two decades but, viewed through the lens of blocs and allies, it lacks the economic heft of the US. More importantly, the dollar's central role in the global financial system is underpinned by powerful network effects that will make it hard to dislodge.

Fracturing is therefore likely to leave the global financial system in something of a half-way house. The complex web of cross-border financial claims that has built up over the past three decades is unlikely to be unravelled to any significant extent and the world will remain financially integrated. By the same token, the rapid growth of cross-border capital flows will slow to a rate more in line with global GDP and within this there may be a shift towards more intra-bloc flows and fewer inter-bloc flows. Perhaps most importantly, while fracturing will lead China and its allies to push for alternatives, the dollar will remain the world's dominant currency and the US will continue to provide the financial plumbing for the global economy. This will remain a source of significant power and influence for the US, which, as fracturing evolves, policymakers in Washington will find increasingly difficult to resist exploiting.

Securing energy and critical minerals in a fractured world

Fracturing will not only reshape the global trade and financial system, it will also have a significant bearing on the broader global economy. It will affect flows of technology, and it will cause governments to focus more effort on securing supplies of energy and other critical minerals. This will have profound consequences for policy in several important areas, including the green transition.

Russia's invasion of Ukraine has already focussed attention on energy and food security in the West. This is less of a concern for the US, which, thanks in part to the shale oil revolution, is now a net energy exporter. However, it has become arguably the most important long-term policy challenge facing governments in Europe.

The European Union imports around $1trn of energy each year, equivalent to 5 per cent of its GDP. Prior to the war in Ukraine, around 40 per cent of the region's gas and just under 30 per cent of the region's oil was supplied by Russia. Russia now supplies around 10 per cent of the region's gas and just 3 per cent of its oil. This has been made possible by a large pivot towards imports of oil from the US, Brazil and Norway, and imports of natural gas from the US. In just two years, Europe's energy map has been fundamentally redrawn.[15]

This is, of course, an extreme example of how geopolitical rupture can affect efforts to secure supply chains. However, Russia's invasion of Ukraine has made clear to governments on both sides of the fracturing divide the importance of securing supplies of critical inputs from friendly countries.

This is likely to spur efforts to re-orientate supplies of other critical minerals towards allies.

This is one area where China holds an advantage over the US. A significant share of the global production of several key minerals comes from either China or one of its close allies. This includes cobalt and so-called 'rare earths', which are critical inputs to electric vehicles and batteries, as well as zinc, which is used extensively in a range of green technologies.

Control over the supply of critical minerals is already being exploited as a policy tool. In September 2023, in response to US controls on the export of chip-making technology to China, Beijing announced curbs on shipments of gallium and germanium, which are used in the production of semiconductors. China is by far the biggest player in the global supply chain of both minerals, producing 80 per cent of the world's gallium and 60 per cent of its germanium. Following the imposition of export controls, the price of both gallium and germanium doubled, raising input costs for producers in the West.[16]

However, while China dominates the supply of these minerals, other sources exist – it is just that until now it has not been economically efficient or politically important to exploit them. The imposition of export controls by China has changed this calculus. The surge in the prices of gallium and germanium has made the development of new sources of both minerals profitable. At the same time, the threat of being cut off from supplies is leading governments in the West to explore the development of sources in friendly countries. Taken together, this will eventually increase the global supply of both commodities and therefore reduce prices.

This provides a playbook for how fracturing is likely to affect the market for all manner of critical, and hitherto obscure, minerals. In the first instance, concerns over supply will push up prices. But in time, this will create new sources of supply that will bring prices back down. The result is likely to be that the push to secure critical minerals will lead to greater volatility in commodity prices rather than a permanently higher level of commodity prices.

Fracturing and the push for technological independence

The balance of power with regard to cutting-edge technology is more even. China has become a world leader in many areas including electric vehicles, batteries and green technologies. In many cases where it is not at the 'bleeding edge' of technology, China can produce second-generation technologies at scale and at a low cost. Its enormous manufacturing sector, coupled with the vast sums it pours into research and development each year, means that Chinese firms are extremely good at 'learning by doing'. According to the Australian Strategic Policy Institute, China leads the US in 37 out of 44 critical technologies, including batteries, hypersonics and advanced communication networks such as 5G and 6G.[17]

China's increasing dominance of the electric vehicle sector poses one of the greatest dilemmas for Western policymakers. On the one hand, the rapid expansion of China's electric vehicle sector means that over the coming years it will be able to provide millions of cars to households in the US and Europe at a fraction of the cost of domestic producers in those markets. It is difficult to see how governments in the US or Europe will meet their commitments to cut carbon emissions without relying to some extent on imports of EVs from China.

On the other hand, these vehicles are so full of cutting-edge technology that government officials now view them as a potential national security threat. In the words of former US Secretary of Commerce Gina Raimondo: 'It doesn't take a lot of imagination to think of how a foreign government with access to connected vehicles could pose a serious risk to both our national security and the personal privacy of US citizens.'[18]

It is uncertain how this will play out but the most likely outcome is perhaps an awkward middle ground, in which Western governments accept the need to import some elements of green technology from China, while at the same time investing in capacity both domestically and in other friendly countries. In all of this, the US will push harder than Europe to sever tech ties with China.

US technological exceptionalism may prevail

With that said, China's technological dominance is by no means absolute. Indeed, despite its lead in several critical areas of technology, the fact remains that most of the major innovations in recent years have come from the US. This includes the development of advanced MRNA vaccines and – most importantly – the new breed of large language models (LLMs) that are at the vanguard of the artificial intelligence (AI) revolution.

Semiconductors lie at the heart of the push for techno-logical independence. On this score, the US-bloc has a clear advantage. China's chip industry has made huge strides over the past decade. It now produces just under 10 per cent of the world's chips, up from virtually nothing 20 years ago.[19] Despite this, however, China is still critically dependent on foreign chips. It spends more each year on imports of semi-conductors than it does on oil. What's more, the world's most advanced chips are made in three countries: the US, Korea and, most importantly, Taiwan – all three of which fall into the US-bloc. Added to this, the production of these advanced semiconductors relies on technology that is also manufactured by US allies, such as high-tech lithography machines that come from Japan and the Netherlands. Over the past couple of years all of the key players have suc-cumbed to US pressure to curb the export of advanced chips and associated technology to China.

If electric vehicles pose a dilemma for several Western governments, developing a reliable source of advanced semiconductors is the major challenge facing Beijing. Even if these chips are used in only a fraction of goods today, the relentless march of technology means that in a few years they will become critical components in everyday goods and, even more importantly, military equipment. Without access to advanced chips, China will struggle to match US technological supremacy.

China's ability to compete at the cutting edge of tech-nology will therefore depend on its ability to work around US restrictions on semiconductors or to innovate past them. It seems likely that at some point China will develop a domestic source of advanced chips. But most analysts believe that the time taken to do so means that it will remain between five and ten years behind the US on semi-conductor technology.

In truth, any such estimates are wildly uncertain. However, there are several reasons to think the US will retain a broad technological advantage over China. In particular, the fact that its bloc is both larger and more technologically advanced means that the US can muster more resources in order to develop new technologies or fill in gaps left by Chinese supply. The key challenge for Washington is therefore one of policy coordination and keeping allies onside. In contrast, China's bloc is both smaller and consists mainly of commodities producers. As a result, it will have to develop these cutting-edge technologies domestically. If the US can keep its bloc together, the chances are that it will remain the world's technological leader.

Winners and losers in a fractured world

What does fracturing mean for economic growth and prosperity? If it is contained to areas deemed to be of strategic national importance then a fractured world need not be one with substantially lower growth or higher inflation.

In sectors where Western governments push for decoupling from China, production is most likely to move to another low-cost centre that aligns more closely with the US and Europe, such as India, Mexico, Vietnam or Poland. Accordingly, so long as these countries form a coherent bloc, they will continue to benefit from efficiencies of comparative advantage.

The movement of some high-skilled workers between blocs will slow, but this is a small part of overall migration flows. All firms will have to adapt to an environment in which geopolitical considerations have a greater influence on the allocation of resources, but this is unlikely to have a major impact on corporate investment. At the margin, a more fractured world will result in lower productivity growth in the US and Europe, but any changes will be small and outweighed by other factors. Meanwhile, inflation in these economies could become more volatile as fracturing causes surges in demand for and supply of different commodities. But the widespread assumption that the end of the globalization era will result in a substantially higher rate of inflation may be wrong.

In contrast, China will find it harder to adapt to the challenges posed by fracturing. China accounts for a bigger share of its bloc's GDP, and the composition of its bloc is less economically diverse. It is likely to find itself cut off from the most advanced technology developed by the US and its allies and will have to develop these products itself. In many areas it will succeed. However, the size and composition of China's bloc means it has fewer resources to allocate to doing so than the US-bloc. Technological progress in many areas will therefore be slowed by fracturing.

This would be less of a concern if China's economy was otherwise in good health. However, the challenges posed by fracturing will add to existing structural headwinds it is facing. China's demographic outlook is worsening thanks to the fall in its fertility rate, a drop that has been exacerbated by the infamous 'One Child Policy', which was only abandoned in 2016. The working-age population is forecast to shrink by up to 0.5 per cent a year over the next two decades.[20] More importantly, there are growing strains in China's growth model. For almost three decades China has invested between 40 and 50 per cent of its GDP. The result is that it now has an extremely large and advanced capital stock for a country at its level of development. Continuing to invest on this scale is becoming increasingly challenging, particularly when the state has started to play a greater role in determining where that investment goes. This makes generating returns on investment extremely difficult. The counterpart to this is that productivity growth is in structural decline.

The solution lies in a package of reforms, a key part of which must involve the centre relinquishing control and allowing the market to play a greater role in allocating resources. But the response to fracturing is pushing China in the opposite direction – the Party has become more powerful and is extending its influence over decisions around resource allocation. The result will be to pull down China's long-run potential rate of growth. By the end of this decade, annual GDP growth could fall to just 2 per cent.

The shape of the fractured world

All of this will have a profound effect on the shape of the global economy over the coming decades. Most analysts argue that it is a matter of when, rather than if, China will overtake the US to become the world's largest economy measured at market exchange rates. In this book I argue that it may never happen, in part because of the consequences of fracturing. China's struggles will bleed into the rest of its bloc. The share of the world economy accounted for by China and its allies has exploded from just 6 per cent in 1990 to around 25 per cent today. It is likely that this now levels out or drops back.

The counterpart to this is that the US is likely to remain the world's largest economy. What's more, while the world as a whole will be worse off as a result of any reduction in economic integration, it is possible that a handful of economies in the US-bloc may benefit from fracturing. Accordingly, having fallen steadily over the past 30 years, the share of global GDP accounted for by the US and its allies will now stabilize.[21]

However, the exact form that fracturing will take is still unclear. The path we end up on will be determined by four things: whether the US remains a leader that the rest of the West coalesces around; whether fracturing can be contained to sensitive areas; whether China changes course and liberalizes; and whether the two sides come to war.

It is easy to envisage outcomes that are substantially worse for both sides. In a worst-case scenario, it is possible that fracturing could result in a hit to global GDP of up to 10 per cent – in excess of that caused by the Global Financial Crisis. The following chapters explore how fracturing might evolve and with what consequences. They set out what is at stake for governments, businesses and households. And they discuss what might go wrong – and what could go right. But before we get there, we need to delve deeper into the political and geopolitical drivers of fracturing.

CHAPTER 2

Where Did It All Go Wrong?

The neighbourhood of Pudong in downtown Shanghai has become a poster child for the changes brought about by globalization. In 1990 it was little more than 1,000 square kilometres of farmland and paddy fields spanning the eastern banks of the Huangpu River. Within a decade it had been transformed into the throbbing heart of China's financial capital.

At its centre sits the Oriental Pearl TV Tower – a futuristic, rocket-like structure that has become the face of Pudong's modernization and China's economic rise. Around it are skyscrapers that are home to international banks, luxury Western hotels and half a dozen or so Michelin Star restaurants. The streets are lined with sleek, modern apartments, and the air hums with the sound of electric vehicles.

But while Pudong has become a clichéd example of globalization's effects, there are countless other cities across the world – from Singapore to Shenzhen to Sao Paulo – that underwent similar transformations. But what is globalization and why does it matter? Moreover, what drove the wave of globalization that reshaped the world in the 2000s and why is it coming to an end?

Defining globalization

Globalization is one of those words that has entered our everyday language but whose meaning is often unclear. An economist – with characteristic obfuscation – would say that it involves the breaking down of barriers so that the global market behaves in the same way that markets do within a country. A simpler approach is to think of globalization as the process of integrating national economies.

This integration can take three forms. One is the integration of product markets (i.e. trade in goods and services); another is the integration of capital markets (i.e. cross-border investment flows); and a third is the integration of labour markets (i.e. international migration). This integration then allows resources to be allocated more efficiently, which in turn should result in greater prosperity at a global level.

Quantifying the extent of this boost to overall prosperity is difficult, but several studies have established a positive link between globalization and GDP growth.[1] Moreover, GDP is not everything. It is a measure of how much each country produces and consumes but it says nothing about *what* we produce or consume. One of the most visible aspects of globalization is that it increases the range of products and services available to consumers. The rapid growth of the Japanese vehicle industry in the 1970s and 1980s put the final nail in the coffin of UK car producers. But the result was that UK consumers had access to a much wider range of better quality cars at lower prices. The UK car industry – and those that worked within it – suffered, but UK consumers as a whole benefited.

The twin fallacies of globalization

There are two common misconceptions about globalization. One is that it is an immutable force and the second is that it is a recent phenomenon.

Carlos Salinas de Gortari, the former President of Mexico, declared globalization to be 'a fact of economic life'.[2] Barack Obama expressed a similar sentiment when taking aim at Donald Trump's promise to build a wall along the US–Mexico border as part of his 2016 presidential election campaign. In Obama's words 'globalization is a fact because of technology, because of an integrated global supply chain, because of changes in transportation, and we're not going to be able to build a wall around that'.[3]

In fact, there is nothing inevitable about globalization. It is easy to think that the relentless march of technology will make distances ever smaller, and that the economic efficiencies brought about by integration will be impossible to resist. But in practice, attitudes towards economic openness have ebbed and flowed over time. Reflecting this, there are many episodes in history in which economic integration has seemed unstoppable – only for it to shudder to a halt and for countries to turn inwards.

A brief history of globalization

The corollary is that globalization is far from a modern phenomenon. The economic historian Andre Gunder Frank argued that it can be traced back as far as the growth in trade between the Sumer and Indus civilizations in the third millennium BCE.[4]

For those of a more modern bent, China began to establish trade networks with the West along the 'Silk Road' during the Han Dynasty in around 130 BCE. These networks connected Asia, the Middle East and parts of Europe and facilitated the trade of everything from silk to spices, and textiles to precious metals. Gold flowed from Europe to China and silver flowed back. Spices such as pepper, cinnamon and nutmeg were exported from India and South-East Asia to Europe, where they were used in cooking and for preserving food. Chinese ceramics were sent to Europe and Roman glassware was sent in the opposite direction.

Several hundred years later, the discovery of the Americas in the late fifteenth century opened up transatlantic trade routes between Europe, Africa and the Americas. This triangle of trade involved the exchange of raw materials, manufactured products and crops like sugar, tobacco and cotton, and, of course, later, slave labour to facilitate growth. Around the same time, European powers, notably Portugal and later the Dutch and English, established maritime routes to the Indian Ocean, reviving the spice trade that had flourished earlier along the Silk Road. And the Dutch, English and Hanseatic League developed sea routes through the Baltic and North Seas. These routes connected Northern Europe with the Mediterranean and beyond, facilitating trade in goods such as grains, furs and timber. This period coincided with phenomenal growth in several trading nations. Between 1505 and 1595, per capita incomes in Holland rose by 70 per cent – a spectacular amount for the time.[5]

Globalization in the modern era

There have been three more recent waves of globalization in the past 150 years. The first started in around 1870 and lasted until 1914; the second came after the Second World War and ran until the early 1970s; and the third is the current one that began around the fall of the Berlin Wall in 1989 and gathered pace in the 1990s. Each was different but, viewed in the round, there are four key takeaways that are essential to understanding the situation that we now face today.

First, there has been a substantial increase in global trade during every period of globalization. In the first period of modern globalization, global exports rose from around 5 per cent of world GDP in 1870 to more than 10 per cent of world GDP by 1914. That's low by today's standards, but at the time was the highest in recorded history. In the second period, global exports rose from 5 per cent of world GDP in 1945 to over 15 per cent in 1970. And in the most recent period they rose from just under 20 per cent of world GDP in 1989 to 30 per cent of world GDP in 2010.[6] Trade is a defining feature of globalization.

Second, while labour migration was a central component of the first wave of modern globalization in the nineteenth century, it played a smaller role in the second and third waves. Measured as a share of global population, migrant flows in the first wave were almost twice as large as they were in the second and third waves.

Third, the wave of globalization in the 1990s and 2000s was an order of magnitude larger in terms of both its scale and reach than previous ones. For a start, it involved many more countries. The first two modern waves of globalization centred primarily on the US and Europe (with the addition of Japan, Taiwan and Korea in the second wave). In contrast, the most recent wave not only included the major advanced economies, it also involved the integration of large emerging economies including China, India, Brazil, Indonesia and Mexico within the global trading system. More than 4 billion people were integrated more deeply within the global labour force. This was an enormous shift.

But the greater scale of the most recent wave of globalization was not just a function of the number of countries involved – the world also integrated in ways not seen before. Alongside an increase in goods trade, there was also an explosion in services trade. According to the World Trade Organization, trade in services increased from about 7 per cent of global GDP in 1990 to 14 per cent of global GDP in 2019.[7] Moreover, as we shall see in later chapters, the most recent wave of globalization also contained a much larger financial element than was the case in previous periods of integration. Between the early 1990s and 2007, there was a six-fold increase in the ratio of cross-border capital flows to global GDP. The fact that this period of globalization has been so large in size and scope means that the world economy has never been more integrated. This has become known as the period of 'hyper-globalization'.

The fourth and final lesson is that the waves of globalization experienced over the past 150 years have each ended very differently. The first was followed by a period of deglobalization, in which world trade, cross-border capital flows and migration flows all fell sharply. By the late 1930s, migration flows as a share of the world's population were about one-tenth of what they were at their peak in 1910. And by 1930 exports as a share of global GDP had fallen back below their pre-1870 level.

In contrast, the second wave of globalization didn't so much end as stall. Exports as a share of global GDP flat-lined between the mid-1970s and the late-1980s. Migration flows also held steady as a share of the world's population. Countries stopped integrating but, in contrast to the 1930s, they did not turn inwards.

These very different outcomes can be explained by the contrasting actions of governments in each episode. In the 1930s, policymakers actively embraced protectionist measures, in part as a means of diverting what little demand there was during the Depression era towards domestic producers. This began with the US Smoot-Hawley tariffs in 1930, which raised duties on over 20,000 products. This provoked a furious wave of retaliation by America's trading partners. Britain imposed a 10 per cent general tariff in 1932 and other countries followed suit. As a result, average tariff rates more than doubled in the 1930s.

In contrast, the backlash against integration in the 1970s and 1980s was far more limited. Admittedly, the Nixon administration imposed a 10 per cent surcharge on all US imports alongside its decision to abandon the dollar's convertibility to gold in 1971. But the surcharge was short-lived. And although a period of so-called 'trade restraint' followed under President Reagan, the associated restrictions imposed by the US on imports from Japan and Europe were modest in scale and scope.

The central role played by governments in ending periods of economic integration means that we need to get inside the heads of policymakers in order to understand why the mood has now shifted against globalization. We should start by unpacking the motivations behind integration that existed in the first place – and why the reality has fallen short of these expectations.

Spreading prosperity – and Western values

Like many momentous periods in history, there was no precise date when the latest wave of globalization began. The start of market reforms in China by Deng Xiaoping in 1978 was an important and necessary step, as was the collapse of military dictatorships across Latin America in the 1980s. However, the key event was the fall of the Berlin Wall in 1989. This was the moment that signalled the triumph of liberal democracy over communism – and with it the promise that market capitalism could provide a path to prosperity.

Economic policy was shaped by what came to be known as the Washington Consensus. This put the market at the centre of decisions over the allocation of resources, and it emphasized the critical importance of economic openness. Trade barriers and capital controls were torn down and multilateral institutions such as the IMF and World Bank were used as vehicles to push liberalizing reforms in emerging economies. In 1994 the 'Uruguay Round' of General Agreement on Tariffs and Trade (GATT) talks created the World Trade Organization (WTO) and with it a mechanism for bringing economies into the rules-based global trading system.

In a speech to the World Economic Forum in Davos in 2000, Bill Clinton gave a clear articulation of the economic argument for globalization. With 5,000 of the world's great and good packed into the Congress Hall at the heart of the

Davos conference centre, Clinton launched an impassioned plea that:[8]

> 'Open markets and rules-based trade are the best engine we know of to lift living standards, reduce environmental destruction, and build shared prosperity. This is true whether you're in Detroit, Davos, Dacca, or Dakar.'

This is not to say that globalization did not have its detractors. Just months before Clinton spoke in Davos, downtown Seattle had been turned into a war-zone as anti-globalization protests around a WTO ministerial conference turned violent and sparked a four-day battle between protestors and police that was the subject of the 2007 film *Battle in Seattle*.

But those pushing back against globalization were on the fringe. A belief in the power of free markets and integration held sway in governments and boardrooms across the Western world. Corporate leaders and heads of government were united in a belief that the market was the best way to allocate resources, and that economic openness would drive higher profits and greater prosperity. Western economies could outsource low-end jobs to emerging economies and move up the so-called 'value chain' of production. At the same time, the opening up of emerging economies would bring billions of consumers into the global trading system and expand markets for Western exporters.

However, the push for closer integration by Western leaders was not only motivated by a faith in the economic benefits of globalization. They also believed in globalization as a vehicle for spreading shared values, and therefore peace as well as prosperity.

The world in the early 1990s was at a geopolitical cross-roads. US victory in the Cold War had signalled the triumph of liberal democracy over autocracy. But while the collapse of communism in Eastern Europe and of military dictatorships in Latin America had sparked political liberalization in both regions, the institutions that supported this process were still fragile. Economic integration with the rest of the world, it was argued, would help entrench democratic norms and Western values. In the words of former US Deputy Secretary of State, Robert Zoellick, it would lead emerging markets to become 'responsible stakeholders' within the global economic system.[9]

The focus of Zoellick's 'responsible stakeholder' speech was China, but policymakers in Europe also used integration – and in particular the prospect of European Union membership – as a means to anchor political and economic reform in the former Warsaw Pact countries in Central and Eastern Europe. Addressing the UK parliament in 1999, European Commission President Romano Prodi said:[10]

'We have the chance to create a Europe in which all the peoples of this continent can live together in peace, security, freedom, justice and equality. A democratic Europe where human rights are respected and the rule of law prevails. An economically integrated Europe which offers growth and prosperity through a single market and a single currency.'

Western leaders therefore viewed economic integration and political integration as inexorably linked. Globalization was as much about the spread of shared values as it was the realization of economic efficiencies.

Not just a Western project

However, globalization was not just a project driven by Western governments. Integration was also driven by a new generation of policymakers in emerging economies.

The first glimmers of reform began in China in 1978 under Deng Xiaoping. Deng had played a prominent role in the revolution that swept the Communists to power in 1949 and had held several senior positions in Mao Zedong's government. But he was also a moderate, whose economic and political pragmatism led to him being purged during the Cultural Revolution of the late 1960s and early 1970s. Deng started to resurrect his career in the mid-1970s and when Mao died in 1976 a power struggle ensued.

Deng emerged victorious but he inherited a moribund economy. Although he was a committed member of the Communist Party, Deng correctly diagnosed that China's economic decline was due to excessive state control over the allocation of resources. He embarked upon a programme of reform that gradually liberalized the economy and permitted a greater role for the market.

At the time, China was a highly agrarian economy and so agriculture was the natural place to start. Deng instituted a policy called the Household Responsibility System, which dismantled collectivization and allowed peasant farmers to sell any surplus they produced. The policy was a roaring success.

Other reforms followed. Not only did these accelerate the transition from strict state control, they also started to open China up to the rest of the world. In particular, the creation of Special Economic Zones (SEZs) introduced experimental grounds where foreign investment was encouraged and export-driven growth prioritized. This was complemented by gradual changes to the Hukou system, which had long restricted the movement of China's rural population. Over time, this allowed millions to migrate to burgeoning urban centres, particularly within SEZs, fuelling the rapid industrial growth. These reforms dismantled the old command economy, integrated China into the global market and set the stage for its emergence as a global economic power.

An export-led growth model

Market reforms were critical to China's rapid economic growth through the 1980s, 1990s and 2000s. However, its model of development has also played a central role in shaping the economy it has become today. It emphasizes investment and production over consumption – and this has resulted in an economy that is heavily export-dependent.

Despite being a notionally Communist country, China's social safety remains extremely weak. For example, per capita government spending on healthcare in China is one-seventh of the average in the Organisation for Economic Co-operation and Development (OECD).[11] It is a similar picture for government spending on welfare support. This creates a precarious situation for Chinese households and means they save far more of their income than is the case in the West. The counterpart of this high savings rate is that household consumption accounts for a relatively low share of GDP, while investment accounts for a large share of GDP.

Rates differ significantly between economies, but investment typically accounts for about 15–20 per cent of GDP in advanced economies and about 25 per cent of GDP in emerging economies, where the quality of capital stock is lower and investment needs are greater. In China, investment has averaged over 40 per cent of GDP for the past 25 years.

The result has been an enormous upgrading of the country's capital stock. Roads, railways, airports and bridges have been constructed on a vast scale. The country's industrial infrastructure has been revolutionized too. In 2022 China accounted for more than half of all industrial robots installed in the world.[12]

All of this has led to a huge expansion of China's productive capacity. And because domestic consumption has accounted for a relatively small share of GDP, Chinese producers have relied on other countries as a source of demand for their production. Exports have therefore become central to China's model of development.

In many respects, China has simply followed in the footsteps of other countries in the region. Starting after the Second World War, economies in Asia followed what became known as the 'flying geese' model of economic development. Integration within global supply chains meant that manufacturing production spread out across the region, moving from one country to another as incomes rose, mimicking the formation of flying geese. Production that took place in Japan in the 1950s and 1960s moved to Korea and Taiwan in the 1970s and 1980s, and then to China in the 1990s and 2000s.

But the scale of China's industrialization is unprecedented, and its integration into the global economy has been much faster than with previous countries. None of this would have been possible if the rest of the world had not embraced globalization. China's entry into the WTO in 2001 was

The Fractured Age

especially critical in this regard. It meant the world's major economies slashed tariffs on imports from China, and it also encouraged multinationals to move operations to China since WTO membership afforded legal protections.

By 2009 China had become the world's largest exporter, and by 2012 it became the world's largest manufacturer.[13] Admittedly, GDP per head in China is still just under 30 per cent of that of the US, measured at purchasing power parity (PPP) exchange rates.[14] But this has increased from just 2 per cent of US levels in 1980 and, as incomes in China have risen, hundreds of millions of people have been lifted out of extreme poverty. Market reforms laid the foundations for China's rise – but it was turbo-charged by globalization.

Latin America's transformation

Economic reform in Latin America started later than in China but came from a higher base. The region industrialized rapidly in the 1950s and 1960s but did so within a model of state-led capitalism. This put the government at the centre of decisions over the allocation of resources, expanded the influence of the state and relegated the role of markets. Most economies in the region were relatively closed, with exports and imports typically equivalent to just over 10 per cent of GDP.[15]

For much of the post-war period Latin America experienced rapid rates of economic growth. However, the region's form of state-led capitalism increasingly went hand-in-hand with fiscal profligacy. This resulted in chronic budget and current account deficits and mounting debt burdens. In the late 1970s the Fed began to tighten monetary policy, setting the stage for a succession of fiscal and currency crises in Latin America, which then bled into rampant inflation.

The military governments that dominated most, but not all, of the region began to fall in the mid-1980s. However, in many ways political liberalization intensified macro-economic instability in Latin America as newly democratic governments kept fiscal policy excessively loose in a mis-guided attempt to appease voters and hold together frag-ile political coalitions that had been united by a desire to overthrow dictatorship but not much else.

By the mid-1990s, public patience was wearing thin and a new generation of political leaders, many of whom had been educated in the US, was coming to prominence. This ushered in a period of reform.

A core component was restoring macroeconomic sta-bility. Fiscal and monetary policy was tightened, bringing inflation under control and putting the public finances on a more stable footing. This allowed currencies to be floated and the subsequent adjustment in real exchange rates helped to restore external competitiveness. But gov-ernments also undertook reforms that promoted the role of the market and liberalized economies. A critical element of this was lifting restrictions on trade. The average tar-iff rate on imports to Brazil fell from over 30 per cent in 1989 to 6 per cent in 2006, while tariffs on imports to Mexico – which together with the US and Canada joined the North American Free Trade Agreement (NAFTA) in 1994 – dropped to under 2 per cent.[16] At the same time, restrictions on inward foreign investment were lifted.

None of these reforms happened overnight and there were frequent wobbles along the way: Mexico experienced a financial crisis in 1994 and Argentina, which struggled to entrench reform to the same extent as other countries in the region, experienced one in 2001. But by the time of Argentina's crisis it had become the exception rather than the norm within the region.

It was a bumpy path but by the early 2000s Latin America had been changed from an economic basket case to a more stable, open and market-based economy.

This provided the platform for a golden age of growth in the 2000s, which was then accelerated by a surge in demand for the region's commodities. Much of this came from China, whose investment-driven boom sucked in vast quantities of natural resources – silver and zinc from Peru, copper from Chile, iron ore from Brazil, soy beans from Argentina. This gave rise to the concept of 'South-South' trade – the idea that exports didn't just flow from emerging economies to advanced economies; in the globalized world of the twenty-first century, emerging markets were also a source of significant export demand.[17]

In many cases, the initial economic transformation of Latin America was supported by IMF programmes, but it was ultimately successful only because of a domestic political will to see them through. And this political will was rooted in a belief that the market and integration with the rest of the global economy offered a path to prosperity.

From communism to capitalism

Impressive though the economic transformation in China and Latin America was, the biggest challenges were faced by policymakers in the former Soviet bloc. Decades of communist rule had brought the region's economy to its knees. According to the historian Tony Judt, a shopper in Washington, DC in the 1980s had to work just over 12 hours to afford a basket of basic foods. By contrast, a worker in Moscow had to work over 42 hours in order to afford the same basket of goods – assuming of course that they could be found in shops in the first place.[18]

Economic decline reflected the extreme distortions created by central planning. As in China and Latin America, newly democratic governments recognized that market reforms offered a path to prosperity. But the starting point necessitated a more radical approach. Aside from a small private sector in Poland and Hungary, the old command and control system dominated. Factors of production were organized primarily to support military prowess rather than promote growth. By the end of the 1980s some estimates suggest that military spending was equivalent to around 25 per cent of Soviet GDP.

Dismantling the old system required the reorganization of labour and capital on a huge scale and, initially at least, it brought about a large loss of output. Real GDP in Central and Eastern Europe fell by around 30 per cent in the first five years of the transition. Accordingly, the initial focus of policymakers was on stabilization. Fiscal positions worsened dramatically as tax bases collapsed and, in some cases (notably Russia), state subsidies were withdrawn only gradually. The region's fiscal problems were compounded by the vast sums of foreign debt that some governments accumulated in the process of trying to prevent the old system from collapsing.

Meanwhile, inflation spiralled. This was due in part to the abolition of price controls and the inevitable drop in currencies as controls were removed. But in many cases (notably in the former Soviet Union) it also stemmed from a fundamental lack of monetary control and, in particular, a temptation to monetize budget deficits.

Economic stability was ultimately achieved in three ways. First, public spending was cut sharply and governments took steps to shore up their tax bases, principally by improving enforcement. Second, monetary policy was tightened and exchange rates were stabilized. Finally, a number of governments also restructured their debts. In some cases, this required substantial assistance from the US and other Western governments under the so-called Brady Plan, named after US Treasury Secretary Nicholas Brady.

The restoration of macroeconomic stability provided a platform for growth. Yet while policymakers knew that they needed to stabilize their economies in the short run they also understood that market reforms held the key to long-run prosperity. State-owned firms were privatized, price controls were lifted and barriers to trade and foreign investment were dismantled.

Each of these reforms was important, but success hinged to a large extent on building the necessary institutions to support capitalist structures. The economies of Central and Eastern Europe and the Baltic states had the most success in this regard. This was in part because they had been thriving market economies before the rise of Communism. But it was also because the prospect of European Union membership helped to anchor the reform process.

Entry to the EU required completing 35 so-called 'chapters' of accession, covering everything from the free movement of goods, capital and labour to the adoption of EU competition rules protecting property rights. From the perspective of governments in Central and Eastern Europe, accession to the EU would unlock billions of euros of transfers from Brussels that would turbo-charge their development. But the reforms needed to secure EU membership were critical to building the structures and institutions needed to support a market economy and thus sustain prosperity.

The results have been spectacular. Average incomes in central Europe increased from \$10,000 in 2000 to \$45,000 in 2022.[19] Prague now has the fourth highest GDP per capita of all EU city-regions when measured at purchasing power parity exchange rates. Five of the EU's top 20 richest cities are from the former Eastern bloc.[20] Integration with the rest of Europe and, indeed, the rest of the world has been fundamental to their economic prosperity.

The spirit of the 1990s

All of this tells us three things about the push to globalize in the 1990s. First, governments in both advanced and emerging economies believed that integration would deliver economic growth and greater prosperity for all. Second, over and above this, political leaders in the US and Europe also viewed globalization as a means to spread Western liberal values. And finally, as integration deepened, it came to be seen by governments across the world as an immutable force. In the words of the former UN Secretary General, Kofi Annan, 'arguing against globalization is like arguing against the laws of gravity'.[21] Globalization had its detractors but, like Churchill's political view of democracy, it was the worst way of organizing the global economy apart from all the others that had been tried. Globalization was a force for good – and resisting it was in any case futile.

History repeats

In fact, globalization is not quite the unstoppable force that many came to assume. As we have seen, the rules that govern the global economy are fluid, shaped by changing power dynamics, ideologies and circumstances. With populism and nationalism on the rise in many economies, and political leaders increasingly pushing back against free trade and open borders, we are once again at a critical juncture.

Many point to Donald Trump's first successful run to be US President in 2016 as the moment when the mood shifted against globalization. In fact, the shift came earlier, in the period between the eruption of the Global Financial Crisis (GFC) in 2007–08 and the accession to the leadership in China of Xi Jinping in 2012.

The 2008 GFC inflicted huge economic pain on the West. The peak-to-trough fall in GDP per head was about 5 per cent in the US, 6 per cent in the euro-zone and 7 per cent in the UK. What's more, the recovery from the crisis has also been depressingly slow and incomplete. By mid-2024 GDP per head was still just under 10 per cent below its pre-crisis trend in the US, 20 per cent below its pre-crisis trend in the UK and 30 per cent below its pre-crisis trend in the euro-zone.[22]

The financial crisis itself was caused by an unsustainable build-up of private sector debt in advanced economies, and the subsequent bursting of the associated bubble in housing markets. The recovery was slowed by extreme fiscal austerity and the need to repair private sector balance sheets. However, the crisis also exposed deeper vulnerabilities in Western economies. For the previous two decades governments had presented global integration as a means of delivering prosperity for all. Viewed through this lens, it did not matter that the US lost 5 million well-paid manufacturing jobs between the mid-1980s and the mid-2000s because new jobs were being created elsewhere in the economy, in sectors such as digital services and the 'knowledge economy'. Overall unemployment was low and consumer spending was strong.

However, the 2008 crisis revealed that rather than prospering as economies moved up the value chain of production, many households in the West had become dangerously dependent on credit and rising asset prices to sustain consumption. It also shone a light on the rising levels of inequality, particularly in America. According to research by the Congressional Budget Office, the top 1 per cent of US households saw a 275 per cent increase in their real after-tax income between 1979 and 2007, while the bottom 20 per cent had an increase of just 18 per cent.[23]

The extent to which globalization is responsible for rising inequality in the West is a source of contention. Branko Milanović, an influential development economist, believes that it has played a critical role. He argues that globalization benefited the middle part of the global income distribution (i.e. the middle classes in emerging markets) and the top end of the global income distribution (i.e. the very richest in the West). In contrast, the gains at the very bottom and the upper-middle part of the global income distribution have been much smaller.[24] The latter includes working-and middle-class households in the West and reflects the loss of previously well-paid jobs in manufacturing to Asia and other emerging economies.

However, other economists, including Dani Rodrik, paint a more nuanced picture. They argue that while globalization has probably increased inequality in the US and Europe, it is not the only factor – and probably not even the most important one. Other explanations include 'skills-biased' technical change, which meant that well-paid workers in the West were better able to exploit new technologies to their advantage, and the liberalization of US and European labour markets in the 1980s, which eroded trade union power and with it the ability of low-paid workers to defend their share of income.[25]

While Rodrik makes the more convincing case, the reality is that globalization provided an easy and convenient scapegoat for the rising band of populist politicians that came to prominence in the West following the Global Financial Crisis. The explanation for rising inequality given by Rodrik and others requires a careful and considered policy response. By comparison, blaming globalization – and by extension foreigners – gave the illusion of an easier solution: simply roll back integration.

Speaking to an audience of factory workers in Pennsylvania during his first successful campaign for the presidency in 2016, Donald Trump railed against politicians who 'have aggressively pursued a policy of globalization – moving our jobs, our wealth and our factories to Mexico and overseas'.[26] He promised to bring thousands of manufacturing jobs back to the US. That promise is as yet unfulfilled but he did levy tariffs on around half of US imports from China and renegotiate America's free-trade agreement (FTA) with Mexico and Canada. Nor was Trump unique in weaponizing a backlash against globalization: concerns about open borders featured prominently in the UK's Brexit referendum as well as in recent elections in France, Italy and Germany.

Democracy's retreat

However, while the costs of globalization have been wildly exaggerated by the populists, it is also true that it failed to meet the lofty expectations set by the previous generation of world leaders. In particular, economic integration did not deliver the political liberalization that many anticipated.

Russia's slide back to autocracy has been extreme but other countries, including India, Brazil, Turkey and Hungary, have experienced an erosion of democratic norms. According to think tank Freedom House, global freedom – a measure of political rights and civil liberties – has fallen for 18 consecutive years since 2006.[27] In all of this, the most important shift has been in China.

China's challenge

The watershed moment came in 2012, when Xi Jinping became leader. Initially, Xi was viewed by some to be a leader who would deepen China's reforms. He wooed Western leaders with promises to tackle endemic corruption within government and large state-owned companies. And the fact that he had previously held senior positions in several economically-advanced regions reassured business leaders of his pro-market credentials.

In practice, economic and political reforms have taken a backward step under Xi. The overriding priority has been to reassert the primacy of the Party in domestic life and to advance China's position as a global superpower. The government has become more repressive at home: pro-democracy campaigners have been rounded up, domestic surveillance has been stepped up and media censorship tightened. At the same time, Beijing has adopted a more assertive foreign policy under Xi.

This is most obvious in its willingness to make increasingly forceful territorial claims to Taiwan. But Xi's geopolitical ambitions extend well beyond Taiwan. Beijing has been increasingly assertive in its territorial claims in the South China Sea, building artificial islands and establishing military bases, despite competing claims from other countries in the region. And it has taken a harder line on Hong Kong's autonomy and freedoms, enacting a national security law in 2020 that grants Beijing more control.

China's challenge to US hegemony has been backed by substantial military expansion. According to the US Department of Defense, China now has the largest navy in the world and the largest aviation force in the Indo-Pacific region.[28] But Beijing has also used its increasing economic heft to develop tools of soft power. The most important of these has been the Belt and Road Initiative, which has been developed as a vehicle to funnel the external assets generated by China's persistent current account surpluses into emerging economies across Asia, Africa and Latin America. Since 2013 China has invested more than $1trn in nearly 150 countries via the BRI, financing everything from rail links in East Africa and telecoms infrastructure in South-East Asia to major ports in several countries including Pakistan, Bangladesh and Malaysia.[29] Not all of these investments have been successful and several recipients of BRI finance are now struggling to repay loans. But even in these instances Beijing has been able to use the BRI as a tool to entrench relations and exert leverage.

At the same time, domestic economic policy has also shifted to accommodate Xi's political objectives. The Made in China 2025 project, which was announced in 2015, signalled this shift to the world. It set ambitious targets for technological advancement and self-sufficiency in ten key sectors in which cutting-edge technology had previously been under the monopoly of the West. National champions Tencent and Baidu have been backed to develop AI tools and large language models; BYD has received help to expand into electric vehicles; and companies like SMIC and Huawei have been supported to develop advanced chips and telecommunications infrastructure. The exact scale of Made in China 2025 has not been made public but support to Chinese firms in the form of state funding, low-interest loans, tax breaks and various subsidies is likely to run into the hundreds of billions of dollars.[30] This has pushed the country to the technological frontier in areas previously dominated by the US, Japan, Taiwan and Europe.

China as an economic superpower and geopolitical rival

In all this, China's emergence as an economic superpower has been key. The US might have been happy to coexist – and trade freely – with a politically repressive China that was economically middling in size, but the sheer size of China's economy and its increasing ability to project its power overseas means its challenge to the existing order can no longer be ignored. China has emerged as a geopolitical and economic rival to the US. What's more, the manner in which it has done so – in particular the widespread use of subsidies and other forms of industrial support – has led to a growing view in the West that China has cheated the system. It was allowed into the club but didn't play by the rules.

The belief in globalization as a vehicle for spreading prosperity and common values has been shaken. One of the few subjects that unites politicians on both sides of the political spectrum in the US today is the need to be tough on China. Even centrist Democrats and Republicans who might otherwise push for integration on economic grounds are arguing for greater caution. Indeed, it is telling that there was no pressure to roll back Trump's tariffs on China once he left office in 2021. If anything, the scope of US measures against China widened under the Biden administration to include stringent bans on technology exports and financial sanctions on leading officials.

The era of hyper-globalization that defined the global economy in the early twenty-first century is therefore over. This is partly because it failed to live up to unrealistic expectations of an earlier generation of leaders and partly because it became a convenient scapegoat for a new generation of populist politicians. But it is mainly because China has emerged as a strategic rival to the US. So how will this rivalry reshape the world? And as it deepens, how will other countries respond?

CHAPTER 3

Mapping Fracturing

With the era of hyper-globalization now firmly in the rear-view mirror, many fear that economies will turn inwards and that the world will 'deglobalize' in the same way as in the inter-war years. As I discussed in the previous chapter, governments across the world in the 1930s erected barriers to trade and adopted measures to protect domestic industries from foreign competition. This protectionist shift came in response to the wrenching pain caused by the Depression and was informed by a belief that the erection of trade barriers would help divert deficient demand towards domestic producers and therefore stimulate a recovery. In the case of the US it was also accompanied by a broader move towards isolationism and a view that focusing on domestic concerns and avoiding entanglements abroad would better serve the nation's interests. This sentiment had its roots in the traumatic experience of the First World War and the desire to avoid similar conflicts in the future.

There are clearly echoes of 1930s-style beggar-thy-neighbour protectionism in some aspects of the current political discourse. Donald Trump returned to the White House on a platform that included pledges to impose tariffs of up to 60 per cent on China. This was motivated in part by a misguided view that tariffs will help narrow America's trade deficit with China. But the pushback against China, both in Washington and in other Western capitals, has also been a response to the perceived threat posed by its emergence as an economic and geopolitical superpower. This threat is felt most acutely in the US given that China's rise has closed the chapter on a period of American hegemony. And it is the geopolitical rivalry between Washington and Beijing that will shape the global economy over the next two decades, long after Trump has left office.

This time is different

Viewed this way, the argument that we are heading into a 1930s-style period of deglobalization looks less convincing. After all, China's rise does not provide a compelling reason for the US to cease trading with Europe and its other allies. Indeed, the emergence of China as a rival to the US may even serve to *strengthen* relationships within the West as Washington seeks to build a counterweight to Beijing's growing geopolitical influence.[1]

Likewise, China has not turned its back on globalization in all its forms. Indeed, in many respects Beijing is continuing to push for greater global integration. Speaking on a tour of Europe in April 2024, Xi Jinping told the assembled press pack that 'we live in an interdependent world and rise and fall together'.[2] His words could have been drawn from a speech given by Bill Clinton in the 1990s.

However, China's continued support for globalization comes with a catch: it is now pushing for integration on its own terms. A good example of this is the Regional Comprehensive Economic Partnership (RCEP), a free trade agreement that China has championed between 15 Asia-Pacific nations. RCEP has created the world's largest trading bloc by both GDP and population but it has done so in a manner that is advantageous to Beijing. It has expanded market access, relaxed rules on inward investment and harmonized rules in areas such as intellectual property rights, e-commerce and environmental standards in ways that are helpful to Chinese firms. Most importantly, it has created a body through which China can influence trade policies and practices in the region to its benefit. It is striking that despite being a free trade agreement, RCEP has done nothing to challenge state subsidies for Chinese exporters.

What we are witnessing is not a broad retreat from integration but a new superpower rivalry between the US and China. This is causing the world's two largest economies to pull apart – or, to put it another way, relations between the US and China to fracture. This fracturing raises two immediate questions for the rest of the world: as this process evolves, can other countries remain neutral or will they be forced to pick a side? And if they are forced to choose, will they align with the US or China?

The allure of neutrality

There are several reasons why most governments will try to remain neutral. For a start there are likely to be economic benefits to straddling both sides. A more fragmented world will be one of higher costs and greater economic inefficiencies. Governments will rightly want to try to avoid this outcome. Doing so will require keeping both the US and China onside. What's more, triangulating between them may even produce some economic benefits. India, for example, has been successful at positioning itself as a potential destination for manufacturing production that is moved out of China, while at the same time absorbing large amounts of cheap exports of Russian energy created by Western sanctions on Moscow.

At the same time, political leaders in other countries may also be wary of being viewed by domestic electorates as subservient to either Washington or Beijing. India is now the world's most populous nation and the fastest growing major economy. The population of the European Union is larger than that of the US. Brazil, Mexico, Indonesia, Nigeria, Turkey and Egypt have a combined population of over a billion people. Sovereign governments of large countries will resist being relegated to bit-part players in a geopolitical struggle between the US and China.

Most importantly, there are clear dangers for other countries of getting dragged into stand-offs between the US and China, the outcome of which they cannot control. Speaking on an official visit to China in 2023, France's President Emmanuel Macron told reporters that the greatest danger facing Europe is that it 'gets caught up in crises that are not our own'.[3] In response, he and other European leaders have advanced the concept of 'strategic autonomy' for Europe – Brussels-speak for the idea that the European Union should act independently in the realms of foreign policy, security and defence.

The contours of fracturing will be decided by the US and China

However, despite the obvious appeal of neutrality it will be extremely difficult for countries to avoid picking a side in US–China fracturing. A new era of geopolitical competition brings with it greater dangers of conflict and proxy-conflicts. Russia's invasion of Ukraine – while not a direct consequence of fracturing – showed how quickly countries can be drawn into taking positions. European governments had reached an uneasy accommodation with Russia following its occupation of Crimea in 2014: some sanctions had been imposed on Moscow but the EU remained dependent on Russian energy and EU companies did business (and made large profits) in Russia. Russia's invasion of Ukraine forced European leaders off the fence. Despite a heavy reliance on imports of Russian energy, Europe joined the US in placing immediate financial sanctions on Moscow and eventually adopted measures that have drastically cut its dependence on Russian oil and gas.

It is easy to envisage how US–China fracturing could also trigger events that back countries into similar corners. Indeed, shortly after President Macron's plane left southern China for Paris back in 2023, Beijing pointedly launched a series of military exercises around Taiwan – illustrating both the limits of Europe's influence over China and the stakes at play. And while Taiwan is an obvious focus of concern, Beijing's various territorial claims in the South China Sea mean that it is not the only potential flashpoint. (Chapter 8 examines the risk of conflict in more detail.)

Yet it is wrong to assume that the two sides have to come into conflict in order to force other countries off the fence. The reality is that the economic, financial, technological and military heft of the US and China gives both countries substantial leverage and will limit the ability of other governments to act with complete independence. What's more, it is wrong to assume that the return of President Trump to the White House means that Washington now views every other country merely as a different form of rival to the US. Several advisers to Trump have made clear that countering China is the key foreign policy priority, and it's perfectly easy to imagine that tariffs or other measures could be threatened against America's traditional allies in order to coerce them into following its lead. Accordingly, the extent to which other economies are drawn into US–China fracturing and forced to choose a side will be decided by policymakers in Washington and Beijing rather than by sovereign governments.

The tussle over the use of Huawei kit in telecoms infrastructure is a good example of the extent of US influence over its allies. In May 2019, during Trump's first term in office, the US added Huawei to its so-called 'Entity List'. This required firms dealing with Huawei to seek approval from Washington in order to purchase US technology. At a stroke, the US cut off China's leading telecoms firm from supplies of advanced American technology. An admission by Huawei executives that the firm had violated US sanctions on Iran[4] had angered many on Capitol Hill, and there were genuine concerns that allowing a company with strong ties to the Chinese state access to US technology and infrastructure could pose a threat to national security. But the move was also motivated by alarm in Washington over China's march up the technology ladder. Placing Huawei on the entity list was viewed as a way of knocking out several rungs from above China.

Efforts by the US to push allies to follow suit were initially met by resistance. Some, notably the UK, argued that China's technological rise was inevitable and so should be managed rather than resisted. Others worried about a backlash from Beijing. Germany, which exports large numbers of cars and machinery to China and whose largest firms such as Volkswagen have substantial operations in the country, was particularly keen to protect its economic interests.

Yet America's allies have slowly succumbed to pressure from Washington. In 2020, the UK banned Huawei and other vendors it deemed a high security risk from its 5G networks. In the same year, France told telecoms operators planning to buy Huawei 5G equipment that they would not be able to renew licences for the kit once they expired, effectively phasing Huawei out of its mobile networks. India's decision not to allow Huawei to participate in trials to build its 5G network was tantamount to an operating ban in the country. And while Germany initially resisted US pressure to move against Huawei, in July 2024 it announced a plan to phase out Huawei from its domestic 5G networks by 2029.

The message from Washington to its allies has been clear: if you want to remain under our security umbrella then you need to remove Huawei from your telecoms infrastructure. This is fracturing in practice.

A similar trend is playing out in other areas of technology. Starting in 2022, the Biden administration introduced several controls on US exports to China of advanced semiconductors and the technology used to produce them. But it also succeeded in preventing non-US firms such as ASML in the Netherlands and Tokyo Electron in Japan from exporting cutting-edge semiconductor technology to China. Once again the message to governments in Japan and the Netherlands has been clear: if you want to remain an integral part of America's technology ecosystem then cut out China.

America's economic and political dominance means it is able to coerce its allies. The same is true of China, whose growing economic and political influence has pulled several countries in Asia and Africa closely into Beijing's orbit. Both sides will, of course, need to exert their influence sparingly if they are to keep their allies onside. But the key question in all this is not whether other countries can avoid picking a side but where the US and China decide to draw the lines of fracturing.

The answer will evolve over time and is explored in subsequent chapters. But as things stand it seems likely that, at a very minimum, anything that compromises national security or technological supremacy will come under the microscope, and that in addition to this both sides will take steps to achieve supply chain security for critical inputs. Governments from Rome to Riyadh are already being forced to decide where they stand in these areas.

Pick a side

If other countries are going to be pushed to choose a side, their decision will be informed by the relative strength of economic, financial, political, cultural and social ties with the US and China. It is already clear how some countries will align.

Economic and cultural ties mean that, even though relations with Washington are at times strained, Canada and Mexico will sit in the US camp. Likewise, strong alliances in the area of defence and security mean that Japan, Taiwan and South Korea will align with the US.

Australia has strong economic ties to China, which is its largest export market. However, these are trumped by a strong defence, security and political alignment with the West. Australia was the first nation to prohibit Huawei from operating in its country and in September 2020 signed the 'AUKUS' agreement with the US and UK which committed the three countries to jointly develop high-end technologies with military applications. Together with its neighbour, New Zealand, Australia is also a member of the US-led 'Five Eyes' intelligence sharing group (the other three members being the US, plus the UK and Canada). Both Australia and New Zealand will align with the US.

The UK had a brief flirtation with Beijing under the coalition government headed by David Cameron between 2010 and 2015. During this period it even went as far as permitting China to invest in critical infrastructure, including a new nuclear power facility.[5] However, developments since then, including the crackdown on pro-democracy campaigners in Hong Kong, a country which had been a UK colony and with which the UK still has close ties, have forced a change of heart. Relations between London and Washington will ebb and flow but the UK remains among America's strongest allies.

On the other side of the fracturing divide it is clear that some countries will align squarely with China. The most important of these is Russia. The re-election of President Trump has raised the possibility of an improvement in relations between Washington and Moscow. But despite this Russia remains more closely aligned with China. Economic ties between the two countries have strengthened in recent years and China is now the largest destination for Russian exports. The two countries are also united by shared political values and similar world views.

Russia is a founding member of the Shanghai Cooperation Organisation, which is an important part of China's push to build geopolitical counterweights to Western influence. And while Beijing has not given full-throated support to Russia's war in Ukraine, nor has it been a vocal critic. All of this places Russia in China's camp. For similar reasons Venezuela, Iran and North Korea will also ally with China.

Shifting sands

But alliances are also shifting. A good example is Argentina. Deepening economic ties to China, coupled with a long-standing hostility towards the US within the country's body politic, has meant that for the past two decades Argentina has leant increasingly towards Beijing. However, the election of President Milei in 2023 has shifted its economic model and political orientation closer to those of the US.

The lesson from Buenos Aires is that the nature of some geopolitical relationships changes over time. The world is fracturing into US- and China-aligned blocs but the boundaries between them are fuzzy and will shift. More fundamentally, while it is already clear how some countries will align in a fractured world, many countries will face difficult economic and political trade-offs if they are forced to choose between the US or China. The rest of this chapter considers how this will play out in five key areas: Europe, India and South Asia, the Middle East, South-East Asia, and commodity-producing economies in Latin America and Sub-Saharan Africa. It then assesses the broad contours of the fractured global economy.

Europe's dilemma

At first sight, the major economies of Europe appear to align unequivocally with the US. Economic ties with the US run deep: America is the European Union's largest export market, purchasing more than €500bn of EU goods and nearly €300bn of EU services in 2023. Financial ties are also substantial: the US has a stock of nearly €2.5trn in foreign direct investment in the EU, making it the region's largest inward investor.[6] Meanwhile, defence and security linkages are strong and are formalized through NATO which provides a collective defence arrangement for member countries. And while the re-election of Donald Trump strained relations between Washington and Brussels, the two regions have shared political values, including respect for democratic norms. Europe also shares US concerns that state-subsidized Chinese exports will undermine its own industrial base. In 2023, the European Union launched several investigations into unfair trade practices by China in several areas including electric vehicles, green technology and medical equipment.

However, Europe's position is complicated. While the US remains the largest market for EU exports, the region's largest economy, Germany, has strong ties to China. China's investment-intensive growth model has provided a large market for German manufacturers. In 2023 they shipped 100bn euros of goods to China, equivalent to over 2 per cent of Germany's GDP.[7] German firms, including Volkswagen and the chemical firm BASF, have also invested heavily in China. As a result, Berlin has been reluctant to participate in any Western pushback to Beijing. One example, as we have seen, is Germany's foot-dragging over Huawei. Another is its reluctance to follow America's lead when it comes to restricting imports of Chinese electric vehicles.

At the same time, China has made active efforts to court several smaller EU states. In particular it has invested more than €10bn in Hungary, building among other things a vast battery plant and a 300-hectare gigafactory for BYD electric vehicles. Of course, Hungary's economy is relatively small – it is about 5 per cent of the size of Germany's. But Beijing has found a useful ally in Budapest, which rolled out the red carpet for Xi on his European tour in May 2024. Since some areas of EU legislation require unanimous support by member states, it is not inconceivable that an alliance with Hungary could buy China some important protection in the event that the EU moves against its interests.

More fundamentally, Europe has yet to define its place in the post-globalization era. While French president Emmanuel Macron and Ursula von der Leyen, the President of the European Commission, have pushed the idea of 'strategic autonomy' for Europe, the reality is that it does not feel the need – or have the desire – to project power in the same way that the US does. This being the case, Europe often finds itself being buffeted by global shifts rather than setting the agenda. For the most part it has been a bystander in the fracturing debate. It is certainly much less willing than America to take strong positions with respect to China and is far more attached to the old rules-based system of global governance than the US.

What does this mean in practice? While Germany will defend its economic interests in China, it is likely that, on balance, these will be trumped by broader economic, financial, cultural and security ties to the US. So if push comes to shove, the major economies of Europe would align with Washington over Beijing. But much will depend on the extent to which the US presses the issue. Will it extend Huawei-style crackdowns to other Chinese tech firms? Will it continue to allow European companies to access US technology while still serving the Chinese market? Will it try to force a harder split with China in areas such as green technology and electric vehicles? And will the Trump administration use the threat of punitive tariffs in order to pressure Europe to take a tough stance on China? European governments will try to prevent the growing rivalry between the US and China from overshadowing their own economic interests, but if they are forced to take a position on these questions, they seem sure to side with America.

India's opportunity

If Europe's position is complicated, then India's is perhaps the most intriguing. As the world's most populous nation and its fastest growing major economy, it will be courted by both sides. From the perspective of Washington, India is one of only two countries (along with Japan) that can provide a significant regional counterweight to China. From the perspective of Beijing, India is a critical member of the BRICS grouping of large emerging economies, which it has sought to build as a bulwark to broader US influence.

But India has a long tradition of non-alignment – that is to say, a policy of not taking sides in geopolitical conflicts. This began in the Cold War, when India chose not to formally align with either the Western bloc led by the United States or the Eastern bloc led by the Soviet Union. More recently, India has maintained what it has portrayed as a neutral position on Russia's war in Ukraine. It has abstained on UN votes condemning Russia's invasion and refused to publicly condemn aggression in Ukraine. Critics, however, might reasonably argue there is a fine line between non-alignment and flagrant opportunism. Imports from Russia have risen sixfold since the start of the war, as India has hoovered up vast quantities of Russian energy made cheap by the West's sanctions on Moscow.[8]

If India were forced off the fence, many assume it would lean towards China. This is due in part to the authoritarian leanings of its Prime Minister, Narendra Modi, who was re-elected for a third term in office in June 2024. However, both geopolitical and economic considerations mean that in many respects India fits more easily within the US-bloc.

For a start, India and the US have a shared interest in limiting the power and influence of China. One important point that is often overlooked by those who believe that China might develop the BRICS into a group able to act as a counterweight to the West is that its two most important members share a contested land border along the Himalayas. To the west, China controls 38,000 sq km of territory that New Delhi also claims; to the east, India holds 90,000 sq km that Beijing says belongs to China.

The dispute has its roots in the historical ambiguities over borders that emerged after colonialism but has now become a matter of national pride. Although the border dispute is mostly peaceful, it has occasionally caused military skirmishes, most notably in 2020 when at least 20

Indian soldiers were killed in a fire-fight.[9] Even if further conflict is avoided, it remains a major source of friction between the countries and a key barrier to strong relations between New Delhi and Beijing.

India is also concerned about China's military presence in the Indian Ocean and its close ties with Pakistan. If India's alignment is uncertain, strong economic ties and heavy investment under the BRI mean that the rest of South Asia allies more naturally with China. This has provided Beijing with a strong footing in the region that has ruffled feathers in New Delhi.

Economic factors also suggest that India will lean more to the US than China. America is India's largest export market, purchasing four times the value of Indian goods and services that China purchases. Foreign direct investment from the US is also around 50 times larger than it is from China.[10] And a larger diaspora of expats in America means that remittance flows from the US to India are substantial.

Finally, aligning with the US could enable India to capitalize on the opportunities created by fracturing. If America and its allies push to move the manufacture of certain goods out of China for security reasons then it is likely that production will shift to another low-wage economy that sits within the US-bloc. Despite its spectacular growth over the past two decades, India has struggled to build a substantial industrial sector. Its manufacturing exports are currently about 15 times smaller than those of China, which is a perennial concern for policymakers given that historically manufacturing has been crucial to sustaining rapid productivity growth in successful emerging economies.[11] If India can capture some of the production that is moved out of China then fracturing may offer an opportunity for it to address its longstanding Achilles Heel and develop an industrial base. But this will only be possible if India can position itself as a reliable partner to the US.

Indeed, there is already some evidence of this happening. Apple has shifted production of its latest iPhone from southern China to a new facility in southern India. As a result around 15 per cent of iPhones are now manufactured in India. Other parts of the supply chain could follow. It's a similar story for semiconductors. India's chip industry is still small by global standards – it accounts for just 2 per cent of world exports.[12] But that has grown from virtually nothing five years ago. Fracturing will test India's tradition of non-alignment – but while it is likely to avoid choosing between the two camps, if pushed it seems more likely that New Delhi will lean towards Washington than it will to Beijing.

Middle East: shifting out of America's orbit

The major economies of the Gulf – Saudi Arabia, the United Arab Emirates (UAE), Qatar and Kuwait – have historically been strong US allies but shifting allegiances mean that the Middle East is now shaping up to be at the centre of one of the biggest struggles in fracturing. There are two fault lines: energy, which is increasingly pulling economies in the region closer to China, and security, which continues to pull many countries towards the US.

The development of US shale oil has transformed the global energy map. America has now overtaken both Saudi Arabia and Russia to become the world's largest oil producer. The flip side of this is that it has become much less dependent on oil imports, including those from the Gulf. US oil imports from the region peaked at just over 2 million barrels per day in 2003.[13] Today they have fallen to barely a quarter of this amount. At the same time, China's rapid development over the past two decades means it is now the world's largest importer of oil and oil products.

This has transformed the Gulf's economic and trade relationships. In 1990, around one-quarter of Saudi Arabia's exports went to the US but today that figure is below 5 per cent. In contrast, exports to China were negligible in 1990 but today they account for around 15 per cent of exports from Saudi Arabia. Investment from China to the Gulf has also increased.

Saudi Arabia, Bahrain, Kuwait, Qatar, Iraq and the UAE have all been recipients of investment under the Belt and Road Initiative. And Chinese investment has helped to further Saudi's Vision 2030 programme, championed by Crown Prince Mohammed bin Salman as a plan for diversifying the Kingdom's economy away from oil. Agreements have been signed for Chinese companies to invest in sectors including renewable energy, agriculture and tourism. Meanwhile, Huawei has invested heavily in telecoms and data centres in Saudi.

Stronger economic ties have also extended Beijing's political influence in the region. China has led the push to invite Saudi and the UAE into the BRICS group of large emerging markets, and both countries have aligned with China in votes in the United Nations General Assembly. Most importantly, from a geopolitical perspective, it was

China rather than the US that brokered the restoration of diplomatic ties between Saudi Arabia and Iran in 2023.

But while China's economic and political influence in the region has expanded, it is telling that the Gulf states continue to take payment for their oil and gas primarily in US dollars and have kept their currencies pegged to the dollar. This embeds the dollar within their economic and financial systems.

Meanwhile, the US remains the major player when it comes to defence and security in the region. Admittedly, China is making a push in this area too. In December 2021, CNN reported that US intelligence agencies had assessed that Saudi Arabia was actively manufacturing its own ballistic missiles with the help of China.[14] But America is a major supplier of arms to Saudi Arabia, which are critical to the Kingdom's ability to defend itself against potential threats in the region, and Washington and Riyadh are reportedly working towards a mutual defence treaty that would commit both sides to intervening if either was attacked. Elsewhere, the US operates military bases across the region, including in Bahrain, Qatar and the UAE.

The fact that much of the region sits under America's security umbrella gives Washington significant leverage. The key question is how America intends to use it. Until now the US has preferred to spend its political capital in the region on critical issues such as strengthening nuclear controls and improving the key relationship between Israel and Saudi. Forcing out Chinese technology from the region has taken a backseat. It is possible that the febrile world of Middle East politics will continue to mean that issues to do with fracturing are relegated down the list of US priorities in the region. If this is the case then the Gulf may find it easier than other countries and regions to straddle both sides of the fracturing divide.

ASEAN: a three-way split

Economic ties and territorial disputes will influence whether countries in South-East Asia align more naturally with China or the US. The result is likely to split the region in three, with some governments leaning towards China, some leaning towards the US and some treading a middle ground.

Several smaller economies in the region align strongly with China. These include Cambodia, Laos and Myanmar. Investment has poured into all three countries under the BRI and China is by far their largest export market. Political ties also run deep. All three governments signed a 2022 joint statement at the UN Human Rights Council defending China's policies in Xinjiang, and Myanmar and Laos maintain close military links with China. They are unequivocally China's strongest allies in the region.

For many countries in South-East Asia, however, terri-torial disputes will frame how they position themselves in a fractured world. These disputes centre primarily on the South China Sea, where Beijing has drawn an infamous 'Nine-Dash Line' around territories that it claims as its own. This encompasses territories also claimed by Indonesia, Malaysia, Vietnam and the Philippines. (See Figure 3.1.)

These disputes are an open wound running through South-East Asia and shape attitudes among governments

75

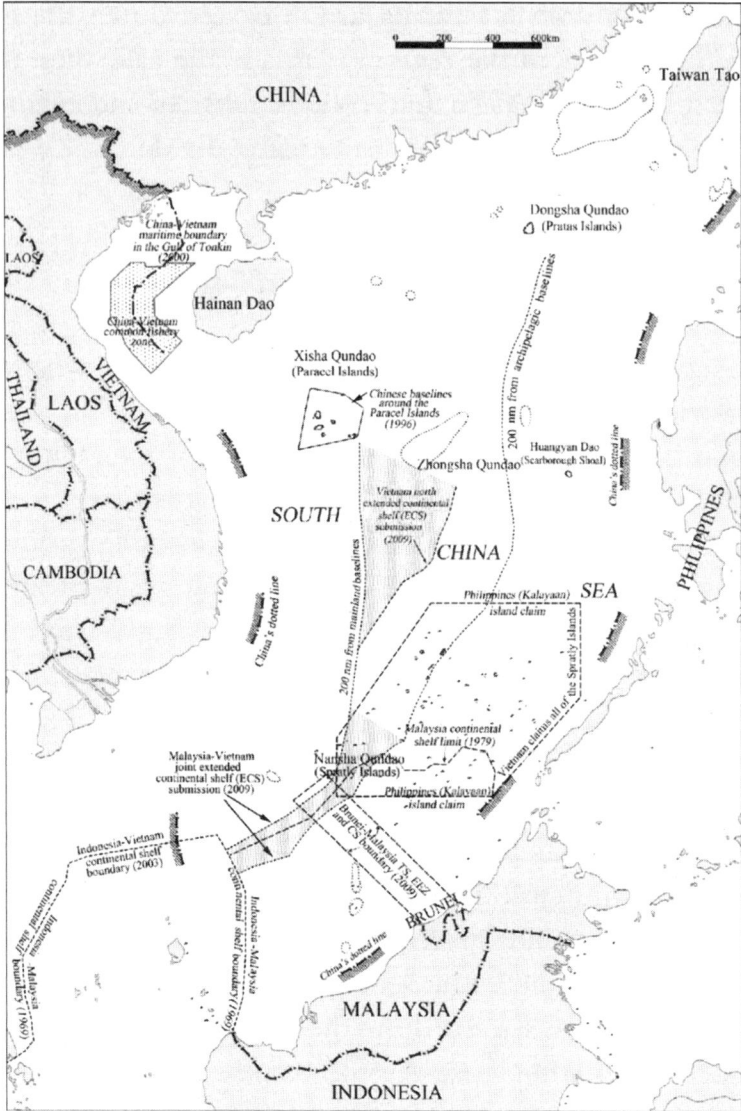

Figure 3.1 Illustration map of the claims of South China Sea coastal States (including the Nine-Dash Line)

Source: Qi, "China's Presence and Challenges in the South China Sea in Recent Years and China's SCS Policies in the Future," 9; Permanent Mission of China to the UN, Note Verbale CML/18/2009; Damrosch & Oxman, "Agora: The South China Sea, Editors' Introduction", 96; U.S. Department of State, Spratly Islands in the South China Sea; United Nations Division for Ocean Affairs and the Law of the Sea, Brunei Darussalam's Preliminary Submission concerning the Outer Limits of its Continental Shelf. Licensed under Creative Commons Attribution 4.0 International.

and opinion-formers in the region. In the 2024 'State of Southeast Asia' survey of key regional stakeholders published by the ISEAS-Yusof Ishak Institute, 60 per cent of respondents felt that China was the most influential economic power in South-East Asia compared with 14 per cent who chose the US. But only 32 per cent said they welcomed China's economic influence in the region, compared with just over 50 per cent for the US.[15]

Anti-China sentiment is particularly strong in the Philippines and Vietnam. In the same survey, 85 per cent of respondents in Vietnam said that, if forced to choose between the US and China, they would side with the US. In the Philippines, 82 per cent of respondents said the same.

The strength of feeling in Vietnam may be surprising given the legacy of America's war in the country and Vietnam's deep economic ties to China today. However, while America's war in Vietnam looms large in Western minds, the Sino–Vietnam war, which came afterwards in 1979, is often forgotten. In any case, territorial disputes in the South China Sea are a much bigger determinant of current attitudes. What's more, although China is by some distance Vietnam's largest trading partner, Vietnam (like India) could exploit fracturing to its advantage if it can position itself as a US ally and attract manufacturing production that is moved out of China for national security reasons. Indeed, as with India, there are some signs that this is already happening. Vietnam has developed a thriving consumer electronics sector, with firms including Apple and Samsung having relocated production there in recent years. Samsung's four factories in Vietnam now account for almost one-third of the firm's global sales.[16]

Meanwhile, the Philippines is America's strongest ally in the region. Rodrigo Duterte, who was Philippine president between 2016 and 2022, did make efforts to pivot towards Beijing. But these were short-lived and the current president Ferdinand 'Bongbong' Marcos Jr has returned to a more pro-US position. The Philippines has a joint defence treaty with the US, claims territory within China's Nine-Dash Line and counts the US as its largest export market. For these reasons it sits within the US-bloc.

All of this leaves a group of South-East Asian countries straddling the geopolitical divide. These include Indonesia, Malaysia, Singapore and Thailand. Sentiment towards the US in Indonesia and Malaysia, in both of which the majority of the population is Muslim, soured in the wake of US support for Israel in its war against Hamas. This may yet be exploited by Beijing to bring both countries closer to its orbit. But Singapore may have more success in remaining neutral. As we shall see in later chapters, a fractured world does not mean a world in which trade and cross-border capital flows are substantially reduced. Singapore may successfully position itself as a financial bridge between the US and China, as well as their respective allies.

Africa and Latin America: strengthening ties to Beijing

The final set of countries to consider is the commodity producers of Latin America and Africa. This group contains radically different economies. It includes Chile, which is an upper-middle-income country, member of the OECD group of advanced economies, and a vibrant democracy.

And it includes countries such as the Democratic Republic of Congo and the Central African Republic, which are ruled by autocrats and where more than two-thirds of the population live in extreme poverty.[17]

However, despite these differences, when it comes to fracturing there is a common thread: they are all major commodity producers. The group includes major producers of industrial metals such as Chile, Peru and Zambia; major exporters of precious metals such as South Africa; major exporters of energy such as Colombia, Bolivia, Nigeria and Ghana; and major exporters of food and agricultural products such as Brazil and Argentina. Commodities form the bedrock of their economic relationships with the rest of the world.

Countries in both Latin America and Africa have built strong ties to China. It is tempting to put this down to a desire to chart a more independent course in the world, free from the shackles of a dominant US in Latin America and Europe in post-colonial Africa. But while this has undoubtedly played a role, a lot has to do with economic structure. China's investment-intensive growth model has sucked in vast quantities of natural resources, many of which are produced in Latin America and Sub-Saharan Africa. As a result, it is now a critically important export market for the majority of countries in both regions.

At the same time, both Latin America and Sub-Saharan Africa have been large recipients of investment from China. This initially came from China's government or government-backed banks, but it has since been formalized through the BRI. This has played a critically important role in building infrastructure in regions where chronically low domestic savings rates constrain investment. Examples include everything from the construction of ports in Nigeria and Peru to the Nairobi–Mombasa railway, which is one of the largest infrastructure projects in East Africa. These projects have provided very visible evidence of the benefits of closer relations with China. Moreover, investment from China has not come with any of the conditions around economic or political reform that are usually attached to investment from the West. For its part, China has been able to extend its influence in both regions and expand the number of supporters it can count on in international institutions such as the UN and IMF.

Yet closer ties to China bring risks for both Latin America and Africa. For a start a growing lack of diversification within export markets leaves them vulnerable to an economic slowdown in China. What's more, because much investment under the BRI has been directed to meet geopolitical goals, insufficient consideration has been given by Beijing to the ability of recipients to repay the associated loans. Some countries are now struggling to service their obligations under the BRI, which in turn has started to strain relations with China. William Ruto exploited concerns about rising indebtedness to China as part of his successful run in Kenya's presidential elections in 2022.

As it happens, it is likely that over time the US will push for stronger ties with both Latin America and Africa as it attempts to secure supplies of critical minerals. Nearly 40 per cent of the world's lithium and three-quarters of the world's cobalt is mined in the two regions.[18] Both are crucial inputs to green technologies, particularly batteries.

Much like the Gulf, a rich endowment of natural resources will mean that Latin America and Africa are courted by both the US and China.

It should be relatively easy for one side to win over smaller countries in both regions with promises of trade and investment. But it will be harder to do the same for larger countries and it is possible they may be able to successfully straddle both blocs. After all, the metals and minerals they are sending to both the US and China sit well down the value chain of production. They are critical inputs to the manufacture of technologically advanced goods – but the value of these goods derives from their design and manufacture, and this takes place elsewhere. Viewed from Washington and Beijing, so long as countries can provide a stable and secure supply of natural resources, they are unlikely to pose a major national security risk. The counterpart to this, however, is that it would also condemn these countries to pursuing a commodities-driven growth model. History shows that this will make them prone to boom-bust cycles, but also that it will make it harder to generate the sustained productivity growth that is key to long-run prosperity. Straddling both blocs has short-term benefits but some long-term costs.

The upshot is that a number of smaller economies in both regions are likely to align strongly with Beijing in the near-term, but over time may be subject to growing pressures from Washington. Meanwhile, the larger economies in the region – notably Brazil – may be able to tread a more neutral ground, but only at the expense of committing to a commodity-centred growth model. Any attempt to develop more high-tech industries would inevitably force them off the fence.

Alliances in a fractured world

The shape of the fractured world will ebb and flow over time as alliances shift. However, as of today, three points stand out. The first is that the populations of the countries that lean towards the US and those that lean towards China are broadly the same. About 3.5 billion people live in countries that align more closely to the US with a similar number living in countries that align more naturally with China. About 1 billion people live in countries that are currently unaligned. In this sense, the world is fracturing down the middle.

However, the second point is that when measured in terms of GDP the countries that tend towards the US are far larger. In 2023, the GDP of countries in the US-bloc totalled around $65 trn at market exchange rates. This was equivalent to about two-thirds of global GDP. In contrast, the GDP of economies in China's bloc was about $27 trn, equivalent to just under 30 per cent of global GDP. What's more, China dominates its bloc to a far greater extent than the US. China itself accounts for about two-thirds of the GDP of its bloc whereas the US accounts for only one-third of its. Eight of the world's 10 largest economies measured at market exchange rates are either strong allies of the US or lean towards it. Aside from China, the next largest economies in the China-bloc are Russia and Hong Kong. Accordingly, the global economic heft of the US-bloc is far greater than that of the China-bloc.[19]

The final point is that the US-bloc is far more economically diverse than the China-bloc. It contains advanced manufacturers such as Korea, Taiwan, Japan and Germany;

rich service-based economies such as the UK; emerging market manufacturers such as Vietnam and Mexico; and low-cost service-based economies such as India and the Philippines. It also contains several commodity producers, including Canada, Australia and Colombia.

In contrast, China's bloc is dominated by commodity-producing economies. This includes major oil producers (Russia, Venezuela and Iran), gas producers (Bolivia, Algeria, Kazakhstan), metal and mineral producers (Zambia) and agricultural producers (Russia and Argentina, although the latter is perhaps now questionable). However, it lacks both the economic diversity and the technological capability of the US-bloc. This will have an important bearing on the economic consequences of fracturing – the issue to which we now turn.

CHAPTER 4

Trade in a Fractured World

The era of hyper-globalization redrew the world trade map. Not only did trade flourish but there was a significant shift in the countries involved. World exports of goods and services increased from just under 20 per cent of global GDP in 1990 to nearly 30 per cent in 2018 – the highest level in recorded history, and well above the peaks reached in the first and second waves of modern globalization. (See Figure 4.1.) But whereas the US, Europe and the 'Asian Tiger' economies of Japan, Korea and Taiwan accounted for about 60 per cent of global trade in 1990, by 2018 their combined share had fallen to less than 50 per cent. Meanwhile, China's share of global trade increased from just 1 per cent to 10 per cent over the same period, while the share accounted for by the major emerging markets of Brazil, India, Mexico, Turkey and Indonesia had increased from 3.5 per cent to 7 per cent.[1] This redrawing of the global trade map was underpinned by three developments.

First, the opening up of emerging economies with substantially lower labour costs allowed production that had previously taken place in advanced economies to be off-shored to developing ones – with finished goods then sold back to Western markets.

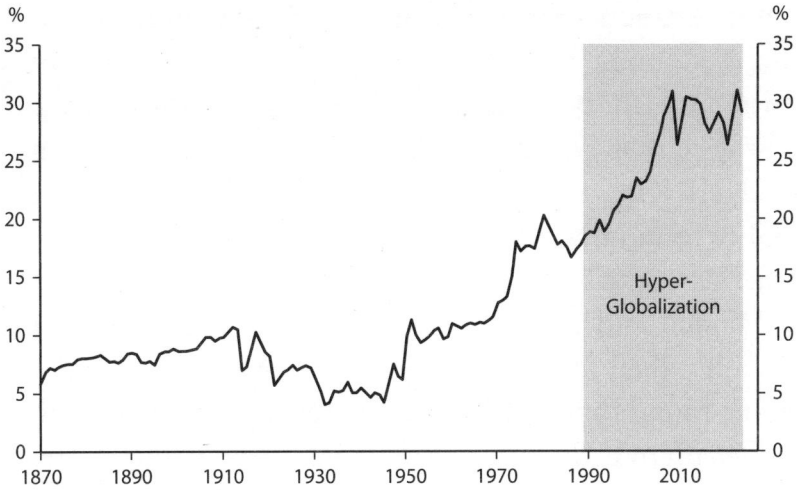

Figure 4.1 Global goods and services exports (percentage of GDP)
Source: Author's estimates based on Klasing and Milionis, 'Quantifying the evolution of world trade, 1870–1949' (2014) and World Bank data: Available at http://databank.worldbank.org

Second, the associated rapid growth of emerging economies created new export markets for producers in both advanced and developing economies. China's investment-intensive growth model sucked in vast quantities of natural resources that created a boom in trade between China and Latin America and Africa. This came to be known as South–South trade.

Finally, advances in technology also facilitated an explosion in trade. This was partly because it became possible to trade different types of goods and services. The information and communication technology (ICT) revolution in the 1990s allowed professional and financial services, including legal, accountancy and banking services, to be traded on a much greater scale.

But advances in transportation and communication also allowed goods supply chains to fragment. Component parts could now be produced in multiple locations and zig-zag across borders as they were assembled into final products. One report by the US Congressional Research Service found that just the seats in some cars sold in North America contained component parts from four locations in Mexico and four different American states, with final assembly then taking place in the US Midwest. The same report found that some vehicle parts cross the US–Mexico border up to eight times as they are assembled into larger products within the supply chain.[2]

No further liberalization

The system of world trade that developed in the globalization era is now under threat from fracturing. But as I have argued, the nature of the threat is uncertain. It is clear that a further significant liberalization of global trade is now extremely unlikely. This is partly because trade barriers are already historically low. According to the World Bank, the average tariff on goods imports was around 3 per cent in 2024, close to the lowest rate since it began collecting data in 1950.[3]

But attitudes have also shifted against further liberalization as a new generation of populist leaders has successfully shifted mainstream views. Reflecting this, the multilateral institutions that led the push towards greater integration in the 1990s and 2000s are starting to fray. The World Trade Organization is facing an existential crisis following the move by the US in 2019 to block appointments to its Appellate Body, which acts as a kind of Supreme Court for settling international trade disputes. As a result, it is no longer able to mediate trade disputes. The weakening of multilateral institutions is important because, with goods tariffs now low, a further push for trade liberalization would have to focus on services. And since services trade is governed more by standards than tariffs, this requires finding common ground in order to harmonize rules. This is notoriously difficult at the best of times, and impossible without multilateral coordination.

Accordingly, while it is possible that some trade deals will be agreed between friendly countries over the coming years, these are likely to be limited in size and scope and may simply update existing agreements, similar to the way in which the United States-Mexico-Canada Agreement (USMCA) replaced NAFTA.

An uncertain future

The crucial question, however, is whether the liberalization of global trade over the past three decades will now be reversed. The re-election of Donald Trump on a platform to impose sweeping tariffs on America's trade partners suggests that there is a real and growing risk that it will. If other governments respond to tariffs levied by the US with sweeping tariffs of their own, it is easy to see how this could tip the world into a trade war.

But despite the heated rhetoric, this is not inevitable. The critical issue is the scale and scope of trade restrictions that are imposed and the extent to which they endure through future administrations. The round of tariffs imposed during the first Trump administration – which were kept in place under Joe Biden – did not have a major impact on global trade volumes. Indeed, both exports from China and imports to the US in 2024 running at close to record highs. This is despite the fact that the average tariff rate on US imports from China increased from just over 2.5 per cent in 2017 to around 15 per cent in 2023.[4] In practice, shifts in exchange rates and efforts to route trade through third-party countries combined to blunt the effect of the tariffs.

Granted, the trade restrictions under the current Trump administration will be more severe than was the case in the first. But it is important to keep in mind that Trump is now a one-term president. And while there is broad support across the US political spectrum for measures to counter China's emergence as an economic and geopolitical rival to the US, there is much less support for a shift towards much wider protectionism. Likewise, while there is growing concern about the consequences of China's rise for economic and national security among America's traditional allies, there is little appetite to increase trade barriers more generally.

The re-election of Trump has increased the risk that America moves into a period of greater isolationism, the economic costs of which would be substantial. (I discuss this in detail in Chapter 8.) But the trends that I lay out in this book are bigger than one man, important though he undoubtedly is. They are being driven by a deepening geopolitical rivalry that will take shape over many years. Accordingly, a reasonable base case remains that over the next decade or so the split between the US and China – and their respective allies – will focus mainly on areas of strategic national interest.

Viewed through this lens there are two things that matter. The first is the amount of trade that takes place between the US and China, as well as countries that align to them. There is already evidence that trade patterns are splitting along the lines of the blocs. According to WTO economists Michael Blanga-Gubbay and Stela Rubínová, while goods trade within geopolitical blocs increased by nearly 10 per cent between the start of 2021 and the start of 2024, trade between rival geopolitical blocs over the same period was flat.[5] Over the course of the next decade, it is the trade between blocs that is most at risk from fracturing.

The second important consideration is the types of goods and services that are traded between blocs. Not all trade is equally exposed. Over the long run, trade in geopolitically sensitive areas such as semiconductors, critical minerals and electric vehicles looks most vulnerable. But trade in other areas, including the vast bulk of consumer goods such as toys and furniture, may be relatively unaffected.

Trade through the lens of blocs

Taking each of these points in turn, the alliances sketched out in Chapter 3 provide a framework for thinking about trade flows between blocs. Using WTO data on trade in goods, we can start to map the key contours of trade within and between the US- and China-blocs – and therefore the

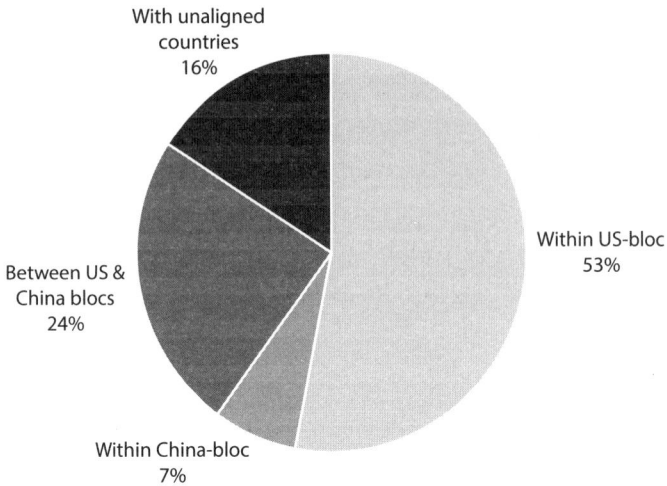

Figure 4.2 Global goods trade between blocs

flows that are most at risk from fracturing. The result is shown in Figure 4.2.

Trade linkages between China and the rest of the world have deepened substantially over the past three decades. But trade between the US- and China-aligned blocs still amounts to only one-quarter of global goods trade. The vast bulk of global trade still takes place within blocs – and in particular within the US-aligned bloc.

The China-aligned bloc is much more dependent on final demand from the US-aligned bloc than the other way around. Pinning down the extent to which this is the case is made difficult by the data. Close to two-thirds of exports from the China-bloc go to the US-bloc, compared with just 15 per cent in the other direction. However, the headline trade figures conceal all manner of trade that is going on further down supply chains.

China's position of 'workshop to the world' means that many products that are made in China for international markets contain components manufactured in the US-aligned bloc. The classic example is the iPhone. It contains components sourced from Taiwan, Japan, Korea and Germany but is assembled in China and then shipped primarily to Western markets. When an iPhone is imported to America, the trade data show the value as coming from China when in reality much of the phone was produced in other countries, most of which align with the US.

One way to adjust for this is to look at trade in what economists call 'value added' terms. This breaks down production across the entire supply chain and credits countries according to the 'value' that they add. This approach suggests that the China-bloc derives around 10–15 per cent of its GDP from exports that are ultimately consumed in the US-bloc. In contrast, the US-bloc derives less than 5 per cent of its GDP from exports that are ultimately consumed in the China-bloc.

This should not come as a surprise. After all, China runs an enormous surplus on the current account of its balance of payments. In 2022, the surplus reached over $400bn on the official data but may have been as high as $600bn according to alternative measures of goods trade published by China's customs agency.[6] Given China's size, the only economy that is large enough to consume the corresponding output is the US. As a result, while the majority of trade still takes place within rather than between blocs, Chinese exporters have more to lose if trade between the US and China is severed altogether.

Small yard, high fence

However, we also need to take into account what is being traded between blocs. A complete severing of trade between the US and China would be an extreme outcome. A more likely outcome is that trade is restricted in key sectors that are considered to be strategically important.

This has given rise to the idea in Western policy circles of a 'small yard, high fence' approach to managing relations with China. This involves significant restrictions ('fences') being placed on trade in a small number of sensitive areas ('yards') but trade elsewhere continuing as before. One concern that is frequently voiced in this regard is that policymakers have not specified the size of the yard and what might be contained within it. But this is not the case. The US and European Commission each launched reviews of supply chains as far back as 2021. This was partly in response to the dislocation caused by the pandemic. But the US review was also intended to make supply chains more resilient to 'other biological threats, cyber-attacks, climate shocks and extreme weather events, terrorist attacks, [and] geopolitical and economic competition'.[7] The last part is an explicit acknowledgement of the threats posed by China's emergence as a geopolitical rival to America.

It identified four areas of concern:

- semiconductor manufacturing;

- high-capacity batteries;

- critical minerals and other strategic materials, including rare earth elements; and

- pharmaceuticals.

The European Commission Review also identified the same four areas but added hydrogen and cloud and edge computing.[8]

Which parts of trade are really at risk?

The fact that there is significant overlap between the studies suggests that there is already a broad consensus among Western governments about the parts of the global trading system that are strategically important and should be the focus of efforts to improve supply chain security. Accordingly, rather than worrying that the size of the yard has yet to be specified, a more valid concern is that it may expand over time as new technologies emerge and economies evolve.

US controls on the export of semiconductor technology to China have been targeted on the most advanced chips, which are currently used only in the production of the most cutting-edge goods. But it is likely that as products become more technologically advanced these chips will eventually be used in all manner of goods, from cars to phones. It follows that the scope of these technology controls will expand over time.

Given this, how can we judge the parts of the global trading system that are ultimately at risk from US–China fracturing? The answer is highly uncertain but it is likely to include anything that compromises US and Western interests in three overlapping areas:

- national security;

- supply chain security; and

- global technological leadership (since this is key to global economic leadership).

The principal concerns around national security are to restrict the ability of a geopolitical rival to sabotage critical infrastructure, access strategically important data and engage in espionage. This will affect trade in a number of sectors. The most obvious of these is defence equipment, but it is likely that Washington will also seek to remove Chinese inputs to anything that involves the processing of large amounts of data (such as smartphones, tablets, electric vehicles) or forms part of America's technological infrastructure. There will be a particular focus on so-called 'dual purpose' technologies, such as drones and radars, which have both civilian and military applications.

One area in which controls are likely to increase is the so-called 'Internet of Things' (IoT). This is the central nervous system that runs through the modern global economy. It contains a vast amount of software, hardware, sensors and processors that enable the collection and dissemination of data required to connect devices and systems over the internet without the need for human involvement. This includes everything from cutting-edge military equipment to everyday consumer devices such as smart watches and doorbells – and it is an area that is dominated by Chinese firms. According to Charles Parton, a Senior Fellow at the Royal United Services Institute in London, Chinese companies now account for more than half of global shipments of IoT modules, providing them with a means to access vast amounts of data worldwide.[9] The IoT has so far been conspicuously absent from the debate around trade security. As fracturing deepens and technology advances, it's a good bet that it will come under greater focus.

The second area of focus will surround supply chain security. This overlaps to some extent with concerns around national security. After all, if an adversary can exploit its access to data in order to attack critical infrastructure then it can do the same to threaten supply chain security. But a more immediate concern in the US and Europe relates to the supply of critical inputs. The one-two punch of the COVID-19 pandemic and Russia's invasion of Ukraine revealed critical vulnerabilities in Western supply chains, first of healthcare and personal protective equipment (PPE) and then of energy. This has focussed attention on other potential areas of vulnerability. The most pressing is the supply of critical minerals needed in the production of everything from consumer electronics to green technology.

The supply of these minerals is often dominated by one or two countries and it is an area in which China has gained a lead on the US and Europe. The European Commission has identified 137 products within its six areas of focus for which the EU is highly dependent on imports from outside the EU. China is the source for more than half of these imports by value. One could paint a similar picture for the US. This leaves Europe, America and their allies vulnerable to any attempt by Beijing either to use its position as a dominant supplier of these inputs to gain leverage over the West or to restrict their supply altogether. Washington and Brussels are now scrambling to diversify their supplies of everything from bauxite to graphite. As I discuss in Chapter 6, the push to secure supplies of critical minerals will be a key fault line in a fractured world.

The final area of focus is likely to cover anything that might compromise America's lead in key areas of technology. This is important because technological leadership is critical to maintaining economic leadership. One consequence is that inter-bloc trade in cutting-edge technologies is likely to fall. Indeed, the US has already taken steps to prevent exports to China of advanced semiconductors and the machinery used to produce them. But once again the logic of technological development means that this push will inevitably widen to include new areas.

It is also likely that Washington and its allies will increasingly seek to counter efforts by Beijing to use substantial state support to establish firms that are global leaders in different fields of technology. This is difficult terrain for Western policymakers, since Chinese firms often benefit from forms of soft support that do not necessarily fall foul of international rules and norms. If the state controls the financial system and supplies cheap credit on beneficial terms across the whole economy then it is difficult to prove that it is providing targeted subsidies aimed at crowding out imports (which would be required in order to justify retaliatory action under WTO rules).

Yet the success of China's approach means that policy-makers in the West will come under increasing pressure to act. Extensive state support has allowed Chinese manufacturers of electric vehicles to steal a march on their competitors in the US and Europe. This serves as a warning to the West. While China now leads the US in several areas of technology, the US retains the edge in critical foundational technologies such as semiconductors as well as technologies of the future such as AI. It is a position that it will now fight hard to defend.

Legislation is changing

Indeed, the three critical concerns for policymakers – national security, supply chain security and technological leadership – are already shaping legislation. The round of US tariffs imposed in 2018 by the first Trump administration focused heavily on areas of strategic importance: solar panels, medical devices and dual-use goods such as satellites were all subject to tariffs of up to 25 per cent.

These tariffs were maintained under President Biden, but his government also oversaw a shift towards a more active industrial strategy aimed at providing support for critical areas of American manufacturing. In 2022, the US passed the CHIPS Act, which included $39bn of subsidies for domestic semiconductor manufacturing and a ban on recipients of these funds from expanding chip manufacturing in China. Likewise, around 80 per cent of the funds disbursed as part of the Inflation Reduction Act (IRA, also passed in 2022) have gone into expanding

domestic battery production. This is a critically important area in which America has become dependent on
supplies from China – in 2023 the US imported almost
$15bn of batteries from China.[10] The IRA also increased
tax credits for electric vehicle production but, crucially,
only if vehicles are assembled in North America and battery minerals are sourced from countries that have a free
trade agreement with the US and are not considered to be
a 'foreign entity of concern'. This represents a clear push
by Washington to remove China from key parts of the
supply chain for EVs.

Governments in Europe have been more reluctant than
the US to take aggressive action, in part because commercial ties with China are stronger. But they are starting
to follow suit. The decision by the US in May 2024 to
levy additional tariffs on a range of imports from China,
including EVs, PPE, solar panels and lithium-ion batteries,
was largely symbolic – of all the goods targeted, batteries
were the only one for which at the time China was a major
supplier to the US. However, the subsequent decision by
the European Commission to apply tariffs of up to 48 per
cent on imports of EVs was more significant given that the
European Union already imports close to half a million
electric vehicles from China annually.[11]

Admittedly, the objectives of the EU have so far been
very different from those of the US. The measures it has
announced have been aimed at countering the anti-competitive effects of Chinese state support, rather than placing a
complete block on imports from China. Security concerns
have so far had less of an influence on policy and, to the
extent they have, the focus has been on de-risking rather

than de-coupling – that is to say, reducing Europe's reliance on China rather than cutting it out altogether. This approach may backfire if at some point European governments decide that they need to remove Chinese technology from certain supply chains altogether – once Chinese firms have gained a foothold in markets, they will become difficult to dislodge.

But the tariffs announced in May 2024 nonetheless marked an important break in EU trade policy. For the past 30 years policymakers in Europe have opened the door to large volumes of imports from China in what are now considered to be strategic industries. The economic arguments in favour of trade held sway in the corridors of power and, since China was by far the most efficient producer, it became the dominant supplier. This has had two consequences. First domestic producers in some areas have been decimated by state-subsidized competition from China. A good example is Germany's solar industry, which was a world leader 20 years ago but has now almost vanished. The second consequence has been that China has quickly developed into a monopoly supplier to Europe in a number of key areas, as highlighted by the European Commission's report noted earlier in this chapter. This has created critical dependencies and single points of failure within supply chains.

Policymakers in Brussels are now taking steps both to shore up supply chains and to counter anti-competitive trade practices by China. They will continue to move more slowly than their counterparts in Washington and their motives remain different, but the tariffs on EVs are the thin end of what could prove to be a very long wedge. It is easy to see how they could expand to include areas such as batteries, pharmaceuticals or military manufacturing.

Firms respond

While the drive to reconfigure trade in critical areas is being led by governments, firms are also taking steps to improve supply chain security. In a survey of more than 100 firms worldwide, McKinsey found that 81 per cent were adopting 'dual sourcing' strategies (i.e. sourcing the same inputs from more than one country) and just under half were developing regionalized supply networks.[12]

These decisions are being motivated more by profit than politics. The supply chain disruption caused by the pandemic was wrenching and created substantial problems for companies across the globe. A key lesson for corporate leaders was the need to diversify supply chains and reduce single points of failure. What's more, the regionalization of supply networks by some firms is exactly the outcome that government incentives, such as those provided for battery production as part of the IRA and the CHIPS Act, are intended to produce. Companies are simply responding to the incentives put in place by governments.

But analysing the motives for these changes misses the point that this is how fracturing will work in practice – it is a process that is being driven by governments but implemented by firms. The most striking aspect of the McKinsey survey is the range of responses across different sectors. Ninety per cent of respondents in the advanced electronics and high-tech sector – which, as I have argued, is likely to be the focus of fracturing – have plans to reconfigure supply chains. In contrast, only half of basic consumer goods firms (such as retail and food and beverages) have plans to make similar changes. The impact of fracturing is real, but its impact is uneven across sectors. At the same time, the majority of respondents to the McKinsey survey expected that efforts to reconfigure supply chains would continue over the coming year. This process has much further to run.

The view from Beijing

I have so far analysed the impact of fracturing on global trade through the lens of the US. But China is also taking steps to increase self-sufficiency in strategically important sectors. Central to this is the Made in China 2025 plan, which was published by the State Council in May 2015. There was an undertone of protectionism in the original document, but it was mostly implicit. Other than an objective to source 70 per cent of core components and key basic materials domestically the emphasis was placed on boosting productivity and moving up the value chain of production. At the time, Premier Li Keqiang suggested that the purpose of Made in China 2025 was to 'upgrade industry … and create new economic drivers'.[13]

The programme was initially welcomed by the international community. Klaus Schwab, the founder and chairman of the World Economic Forum in Davos, said it would help China become 'the leader in the fourth industrial revolution'.[14] However, the mood has since soured as the extent of China's ambitions – and its ability and willingness to deploy state resources to achieve them – has become clear. The Made in 2025 plan was accompanied by a so-called 'Roadmap'. While not an official document, this was produced by the National Manufacturing Strategy Advisory Committee, a government think tank, and has since been acknowledged by the leadership as a key input to its policy framework.

The initial version of the Roadmap contained several explicit targets for self-sufficiency across a wide range of industries, from strategic minerals and medical devices to machine tools and communication networks. However, subsequent updates to the Roadmap have both increased and widened the scope of the targets. They now cover areas such as food processing and household appliances. What's more, they set explicit targets to be a 'global leader' in several fields. For example, for electric vehicles the goal is to develop a self-sufficient domestic supply chain and have two firms in the global top ten by 2025.

The broadening out of the Made in China 2025 plan partly reflects a view among the Chinese leadership that the country lags its competitors in many areas and needs to catch up. But the deepening rivalry with the US and its allies has also played a role. There is a striking overlap between the areas that have received most attention in Made in China 2025 and those in the US and EU reports on supply chain security. And some parts of the Chinese government have even gone as far as to acknowledge there is a link to national security. In September 2022, the Central Commission for Comprehensively Deepening Reform, which is one of China's most authoritative economic policymaking bodies, said that the country's 'national defence' required research into 'core technologies relating to oil and natural gas, key raw materials, high-end chips and to accelerate breakthroughs in medicine'.[15] Efforts to 'de-risk' supply chains are not only being pursued by the US and its allies. China is taking big steps in this direction too – and its push is arguably more advanced than that of Western governments.

China's push to reform global trade

China's efforts to secure supply chains form part of a broader attempt to reshape the global trade system to its advantage. Central to this is a drive to construct a China-centric network of bilateral and regional free trade agreements with the 'Global South' – the loose collection of countries in Asia, Africa and Latin America with which China has built ties through the Belt and Road Initiative. These FTAs typically comprise three elements: market access at low or zero tariffs, common agreements on standards, and rules to promote direct investment flows.

The push to agree FTAs has been motivated in part by China's ambition to position itself as a defender of global free trade in the face of rising US protectionism. But it primarily reflects concerns in Beijing that the global trade system that underpinned China's rapid development is starting to fray and was in any case designed to benefit the Western interests. Policymakers in Beijing believe they must build an alternative system that is both more resilient and better serves China's own interests.

At first sight, they have been remarkably successful. China has now signed FTAs with nearly 30 countries that cover about 40 per cent of its exports.[16] The centrepiece, as I noted in Chapter 3, is the Regional Comprehensive Economic Partnership, a vast FTA covering the major economies in Asia-Pacific. Its signatories account for around one-third of global GDP. Further deals in Africa and the Middle East are planned but not yet completed. Significantly, none of China's FTAs includes the US or countries within the EU.

China has also had success in influencing global standards, which is an arcane but critically important part of the architecture governing world trade. These standards cover everything from packaging, labelling and shelf-life conditions, to safety testing and certification, to the rules governing 5G communication systems. If a country can influence these standards it can also influence the rules regulating global trade.

The setting of standards is typically coordinated by one of two bodies: the International Organization for Standardization (ISO) and the International Electrotechnical Commission (IEC). China's influence on both is growing. According to the US–China Business Council, the number of Chinese-occupied secretariat positions in technical committees and subcommittees, which are responsible for drafting and updating standards, at both the ISO and the IEC increased by around 70 per cent between 2011 and 2020.[17] This gives further support to the idea that China is starting to exert greater influence over the governance of global trade.

However, it takes a big leap to reach the conclusion that China will successfully reshape world trade on its own terms. In fact, China's export prowess limits rather than increases its leverage over other countries.

Because it exports far more than it imports, China continues to run a large current account surplus on its balance of payments. As we have seen, there is some debate as to the true size of the surplus but, depending on which measure is used, it is equivalent to between 0.5 per cent and 0.7 per cent of global GDP. This represents an excess of production that must be consumed by someone else – and the only country capable of absorbing a surplus on this scale is the US. Some point to the rapid growth of trade with the 'Global South' as evidence that other large markets exist for Chinese exporters. However, China's exports to these economies are often semi-finished goods that are ultimately destined for the US. China's global influence is undoubtedly growing. But as the world's largest consumer, America holds the balance of power and will ultimately dictate whether and on what terms it is willing to buy these goods.

The future of world trade

So what does all this mean for the future of world trade? The critical question is what share of world trade will be affected by fracturing. This is an inherently difficult question to answer, not least because it is unclear how deep or how wide global fracturing might be. But that should not stop us from giving it a go.

Around 75 per cent of global goods trade takes place within either the US- or China-bloc, or with unaligned countries. Some trade between the US and its allies, including Mexico and Europe, will be subject to increased restrictions during a second Trump administration. But the experience of the first

Trump administration shows that these would need to be set at severe levels for a sustained period in order to have a significant impact on trade flows. And over the long run, the fundamental drivers of fracturing mean that the focus will fall primarily on the 25 per cent of global trade that takes place between blocs. Of this, the goods that are most likely to be affected are those deemed to be strategically important. In this chapter I have argued that this will include anything that could compromise national security, supply chain security or technological leadership. This is most likely to cover trade in:

- high-tech electronics and component parts, including advanced semiconductors;

- pharmaceuticals and medical products;

- green technologies, including batteries;

- dual-use goods (i.e. those with military and civilian applications); and

- critical minerals.

As Table 4.1 shows, in 2023, goods trade between the US- and China-aligned blocs in these areas totalled $2.95trn. This is a considerable sum. But keep in mind that this represents the upper bound of the trade flows that are vulnerable to fracturing. Moreover, it must be viewed in the context of total global goods trade of $19.5trn in 2023. Put another way, about 15 per cent of total trade (by value) might be affected by fracturing. The impact on supply chains in these

Table 4.1 Trade in strategic goods by bloc (US$ bn, 2023)

Categories	Between US & China Blocs	With Unaligned Countries	Within US & China Blocs	Total
High-Tech Electronics & Component Parts	1210	1018	2917	5145
Green tech	350	170	1219	1739
Pharmaceuticals and Medical Products	325	184	1421	1930
Dual-Use Goods	593	493	1906	2993
Critical Minerals	474	432	1088	1994
Strategic Goods	2954	2297	8551	13801
Non-Strategic Goods	1330	917	3488	5735
Total	4284	3214	12039	19536

Source: UNCOMTRADE, Author's calculations; totals may not sum due to rounding

areas will be substantial. But the vast majority of global trade – at least 85 per cent – will be subject to little or no additional restrictions and it is likely that much of this will be broadly unaffected by US–China fracturing.

Reshoring will remain a populist's pipe dream

Accordingly, a key message from this book is that fracturing will not necessarily result in a major pullback in global trade. What's more, in instances where fracturing does lead to production being moved out of China for geo-strategic reasons, there are good reasons to doubt that it will result in it moving back to the US or, for that matter, to any other high-income country.

It has become common for politicians to seduce voters with promises to rebuild domestic manufacturing sectors. It seems that anybody wishing to be elected today in Europe, and particularly in the US, must pledge to oversee a manufacturing renaissance. These promises feed off a nostalgia for a time when tens of millions of workers in the US and Europe were employed in well-paid manufacturing jobs. But as I have argued, the destruction of these jobs is not just a result of globalization. Moreover, China's emergence as a strategic rival to the US does not in itself justify the reshoring of output back to America or other advanced Western economies.

I have argued that where there is a push to move production out of China it will be for one of three reasons: to defend national security; to protect supply chain security; or to maintain technological leadership. In a handful of instances this might involve some production moving back to the US. But while these cases will grab the headlines, it is a good bet that they will be the exception rather than the rule.

The story of Foxconn in Wisconsin, which I told in Chapter 1, provides a salutary lesson in the difficulties of reshoring jobs. One reason is that the economics are, to say the least, extremely challenging. Wages in the US manufacturing sector are about seven times higher than they are in China and 20 times higher than in India.[18] Moving jobs back to America would impose a significant increase in firms' costs, which in turn would be passed through to prices. For this reason, while there has been a steady flow of companies moving production out of China, very little of this has moved back to America. The number of workers employed in US manufacturing in 2024 was around 750,000 lower than in 2007, and 4 million lower than in 2000.[19] Instead, where production has shifted, it has gone to other emerging economies that align more closely with the US. Apple has moved production of its iPhone from China to India and Samsung has moved parts of its production chain to Vietnam.

The US and other advanced economies may have some success in reshoring jobs in high-skill or capital-intensive sectors, such as chip technology. But over the next decade or so I doubt that we will witness the reshoring of manufacturing jobs on the scale promised by populist politicians.

Trade in a fractured world

Where does it leave us? While the situation is clearly fluid, there are three broad points we can make about US–China fracturing and the future of global trade.

The first is that every country would lose if there was a complete halt to trade, but given its heavy reliance on export demand from the US-bloc, China would stand to lose most. It is for this reason that Beijing is attempting to build an alternative trade architecture that is better insulated from US influence. Yet while it has succeeded in bringing greater influence to bear in some areas, notably trade standards, China's vast current account surplus means that it will struggle to fundamentally reshape the global trading system on its own terms. As the world's consumer of last resort, the balance of power in this regard will lie with America.

The second point is that, as things stand, a fractured world will not necessarily be one with substantially lower trade flows. President Trump's return to the White House has raised the spectre of a new global trade war. This threat should be taken seriously. But some perspective is also required: Trump is constitutionally limited to one more term and there is limited support for a wider trade war in other countries (or indeed across the US political spectrum). Where a consensus does exist is on the need to cut ties with China in areas of strategic importance. While the US and Europe are moving at different speeds and for different reasons, governments in both have identified similar areas of concern: telecommunications, high-end semiconductors, batteries and other green technologies, critical minerals and pharmaceuticals. On the other side, China is making a push for self-sufficiency in similar fields. These are the parts of the global trading system that are most at risk from fracturing. And while the relentless march of technology will widen the scope of government concerns over time, the amount of inter-bloc trade affected by fracturing is still likely to account for a relatively small share of overall global trade.

Finally, even if concerns around fracturing lead to production moving out of China, the likelihood of it being 'reshored' to the US and other advanced economies is low. A more likely outcome is that it moves to another low-cost economy that aligns more closely with the US. This will create opportunities for emerging markets that sit within the US-bloc. While the path ahead will undoubtedly be bumpy, the experience of India, Mexico and Vietnam over the past decade, including during the first Trump administration, illustrates the point: exports from all three countries to the US hit a record high in 2022.[20]

All of this will involve trade. The surge in world trade during the era of hyper-globalization is over. But at the same time, the drivers of fracturing do not suggest a collapse in world trade is coming either. A more likely outcome is that, having shot up in the 1990s and 2000s, trade as a share of global GDP now levels out.

The impact of fracturing on global trade will therefore be more nuanced than many of the more extreme headlines suggest. Yet trade is only one channel through which fracturing will impact the global economy. Over the past four decades the world has also become more financially integrated. Will US–China fracturing lead to a rollback of financial globalization?

CHAPTER 5

Fracturing, Finance and Global Capital

The defining feature of the period of hyper-globalization that reshaped the global economy from the 1990s onwards was its breadth. The world had experienced waves of globalization before but these were characterized mainly by a rise in international trade and, to a lesser extent, migration flows. The latest wave of globalization added a third significant element: cross-border capital flows.

Between 1990 and 2018 there was a five-fold increase in international bond and equity flows, and a seven-fold increase in foreign direct investment flows. Having invested their pensions in US and European stock markets for decades, Western households began to invest some of their assets in rapidly expanding emerging economies, including China, Brazil, India and Russia. At the same time, as emerging economies became export powerhouses they recycled their resulting trade surpluses back into Western financial markets. Financial liberalization in the US and Europe also led to a surge in capital flows between advanced economies.

All told, global capital flows increased from around 3 per cent of world GDP in the early 1990s to over 20 per cent of world GDP in 2007.[1] In addition to the globalization of production, the world experienced the globalization of finance.

A new form of globalization

It wasn't always this way. The world did experience a rise in cross-border capital flows during the first wave of modern globalization, between 1870 and 1914, but these were modest by today's standards. And for most of the 75 years between the outbreak of the First World War in 1914 and the fall of the Berlin Wall in 1989, global capital flows remained relatively limited.

That started to change in the 1990s. The surge in international capital flows over the following two decades was consistent with the 'Washington Consensus' that shaped the global policy architecture: it was argued that, just as openness to trade should lead to greater efficiency in the global allocation of productive resources, so openness to financial flows should lead to the more efficient allocation of global capital.

However, the globalization of finance was underpinned by two other developments. The first was a shift in attitudes towards the conduct of monetary and exchange rate policy, and the second was the development of new technologies that reduced the cost and time taken to transfer capital across borders.

The twin roots of financial integration

The choice of macroeconomic policy regime for any given country is governed by the idea of the 'impossible trinity' that was developed by the economists John Fleming and Robert Mundell. This states that a country cannot have all three of the following policies:

- full and complete openness to global capital flows;

- a fixed exchange rate; and

- independent monetary policy geared towards domestic objectives.

The architects of the Bretton Woods system of global economic governance that emerged after the Second World War took the view that unregulated capital flows posed a risk to global financial stability. John Maynard Keynes was a particularly vocal sceptic and advocated for a system of controls to both manage and restrict cross-border capital flows. The Bretton Woods system that lasted from 1944 to 1971 was therefore built on a system of fixed but adjustable exchange rates combined with global capital controls. Consistent with the trilemma, this allowed monetary policy in the world's major economies to diverge and be set according to domestic needs.

However, by the time of the 1980s, views were starting to shift. The collapse of the Bretton Woods system in the early 1970s, and the painful devaluations required in some countries to restore external competitiveness, had diminished the appeal of fixed exchange rates. A consensus began to emerge that allowing currencies to 'free float' would provide a safety valve through which necessary changes in the real exchange rate could happen in a more gradual and less disruptive manner. At the same time, the scars left by rampant inflation in the 1970s meant that maintaining price stability through strict inflation targets became a cornerstone of monetary policy. This required that interest rates be set according to domestic objectives.

Accordingly, by the early 1990s the broadly accepted view among policymakers and academics was that the optimal macroeconomic policy framework should consist of a) a floating exchange rate and b) independent monetary policy focussed on maintaining a low and stable rate of inflation. This meant that for the first time in 60 years at least some element of capital mobility was possible without violating the trilemma.

This was seized upon by a new generation of policymakers with a deep-seated faith in the benefits of liberalization and openness. The controls that had restricted the international movement of capital since the Second World War were slowly dismantled. In emerging economies, this was often a condition of IMF programmes that were required after a spate of balance of payments and debt crises in the 1980s and 1990s. Everywhere from Latin America to Eastern Europe, and Asia to Africa, loosened restrictions on international capital flows.

What's less appreciated, however, is the extent to which capital controls were also dismantled in advanced economies. In Europe, capital mobility was a key pillar of the 'four freedoms' that underpinned EU membership. In the US, successive administrations from President Reagan onwards took steps to deregulate the financial sector. As a result, there was a substantial and widespread relaxation on restrictions in cross-border financial flows. The shackles on global finance had been lifted.

Technology plays its part (again)

This shift in philosophical approach came alongside the rapid development of new technologies that dramatically reduced the cost and time taken to move capital across borders. This manifested itself in several ways. The spread of the internet permitted the development of online trading platforms that made it quicker and easier for retail investors to move savings into funds spanning different corners of the world. Meanwhile, the shift to electronic trading within financial institutions meant that the time taken to execute international trades fell from days to milliseconds. And the development of digital payment systems facilitated the rapid processing of cross-border transactions through organizations such as SWIFT, the global financial messaging system, at a dramatically lower price. Research by McKinsey found that the cost of moving funds across borders had been reduced from 5–10 per cent of the transfer amount in the 1980s to 0.5–2 per cent in the mid-2010s.[2]

If the shift in philosophical approach to macroeconomic management opened the door to greater global capital flows, then the rapid development of technology forced it wide open. And because financial integration was consistent with the spirit of the time, which emphasized the importance of liberalization and openness, it was embraced by governments across the world – thus turbo-charging the surge in international capital flows.

The dangers of unfettered global capital flows

As with the globalization of production, the globalization of finance brought costs as well as benefits. Indeed, in some respects the costs were ultimately much greater. The dismantling of global capital controls, which had contained cross-border financial flows in previous waves of globalization, came alongside broader liberalization of the financial system. Financial integration therefore went hand-in-hand with rapid growth in the size and complexity of the banking system, a huge expansion of credit, and the development of increasingly exotic financial instruments – all of which contributed to the 2008 Global Financial Crisis.

It is difficult to disentangle the exact role that financial globalization played in the events of 2008, but there is little doubt that it played a critical role in both sowing the seeds of the crisis and amplifying its effects.[3] The ease with which capital could cross borders was a crucial factor in the development of global trade and financial imbalances that underpinned the crisis. Large and persistent current account surpluses run by countries including China, Russia, Saudi Arabia and Germany were re-invested in countries such as the US, UK, Spain and Greece – requiring them to run large current account deficits. These current account imbalances led to the extensive build-up of international assets (by surplus countries) and liabilities (by deficit countries).

The accumulation of external liabilities in effect permitted the US and other deficit countries to live beyond their means. One way this manifested itself was in a period of easy credit and the inflation of asset price bubbles, particularly in housing. Once these bubbles burst, the subsequent freezing of the global financial system led to what economists term a 'sudden stop' in capital flows – thereby contributing to the acute financial instability that followed.

Not all bad news

However, while most economists agree that financial globalization played a crucial role in facilitating the build-up of global financial imbalances that underpinned the GFC, and that financial integration helped to spread risky lending practices across borders, financial globalization has also brought material benefits.

For a start, it has increased the global pool of capital available to firms for investment. The core purpose of finance is to intermediate between savers and borrowers. This is true both within countries and at an international level. For countries that suffer from a low domestic savings rate – notably the US and UK but also low- and middle-income countries including Brazil, South Africa and Nigeria – the only way to finance substantial investment is to borrow from overseas. The problem in the run-up to the 2008 Global Financial Crisis was that this was done in an excessive manner and much of the overseas borrowing financed consumption rather than productive investment. But this reflected a failure of policy making, and in particular a misguided belief in the benefits of financial deregulation and unfettered global capital flows, rather than an inherent problem with cross-border financial integration itself.

Financial globalization has also underpinned the regeneration of global cities, notably New York and London, as well as the development of new financial hubs, such as Dubai. The population of both New York and London had fallen steadily throughout the 1970s and early 1980s as deindustrialization decimated traditional areas of employment in manufacturing and fuelled urban decay. But the development of financial sectors coincided with an upturn in fortunes for both cities in the 1990s. People started to move back, and by the mid-2000s the population of London had returned to its level in 1970, while the population of New York was 12 per cent larger than it was in 1970. By 2020, financial services accounted for about one-fifth of economic activity in London.[4] The revival of London and New York would not have been possible, or at least would have been much harder to achieve, without financial globalization.

Finally, irrespective of the costs and benefits of financial globalization, there is no doubt that it has had enormous geopolitical consequences. Because cross-border capital flows are denominated overwhelmingly in dollars, it has placed the US at the heart of an internationally connected financial system. At some point, a transaction that is denominated in dollars is likely to touch the US financial system. In effect, America has wound up providing the financial plumbing for the global economy. This has conferred an enormous amount of geopolitical power on the US. And as the sanctions unleashed on Russia in the wake of its invasion of Ukraine demonstrate, it is something that Washington has become increasingly willing to exploit.

The global financial map

The fracturing of the global economy has called into question the durability of financial globalization. Will the world remain financially connected or are we facing a rollback of financial integration? And if we are, what will be the consequences? In order to assess all of this we must first establish the true extent of global financial integration over the past 40 years. This requires mapping where capital has flowed to and from, and the effect this has had on the stock of international assets and liabilities held by different countries.

The first point to note is that there is already some evidence that financial globalization has slowed. Measured as a share of world GDP, gross global capital flows have fallen from a peak of 20 per cent in 2007 to around 5 per cent in recent years.[5] On this measure at least, the heyday of financial globalization came in the years before the GFC and ended well before the onset of US–China fracturing.

The GFC delivered a near-fatal blow to the global financial system, and both regulators and bank executives emerged at least somewhat chastened. Stricter capital and liquidity requirements on major international banks have since constrained cross-border activity and many globally active banks have retrenched their business models by focussing on domestic markets. The crisis also dented the 'Washington Consensus' belief in the benefits of financial deregulation and unfettered global capital flows. Even the IMF now routinely warns about the destabilizing effects of flighty capital flows and in some circumstances advocates for forms of controls.[6] Given the role that excessive financial liberalization and large-scale cross-border capital flows played in seeding the GFC, this should be regarded as a positive development.

But while financial globalization has clearly slowed, it is by no means dead. For one thing, measured as a share of world GDP, global capital flows are still substantially larger than they were in the 1980s. Policymakers have rightly taken a more cautious approach to financial liberalization, but with the exception of China most major economies have maintained open capital accounts. There has been no push to resurrect the extensive capital controls that were a defining feature of the Bretton Woods system of global economic governance during the post-war years.

What's more, because capital has continued to flow across borders, the stock of outstanding financial claims between countries has continued to rise. In 2011 these stood at $110trn, but by 2022 they had risen to over $190trn.[7] This is the best measure of financial integration – and it shows that the global financial system remains deeply interconnected.

The consequences of Chinese savings

This partly reflects a deepening of financial ties between China and the US. China's growth model is often described as being 'export-orientated'. While this is true in one sense, the underlying reason for this is that it has an extremely high savings rate. In 2023, national savings were equivalent to just under 44 per cent of GDP.[8] The counterpart to this high savings rate has been a low level of consumption when measured as a share of GDP, which in turn has meant that China has become dependent on the rest of the world (i.e. exports) as a source of demand. As a result, it has run large and persistent trade and current account surpluses on its balance of payments, meaning that it has accumulated significant international assets. These totalled nearly $10trn in 2023.[9] The only country with financial markets that are deep and liquid enough to absorb foreign inflows on this scale is America – hence the consequence of China's low savings rate and export-oriented growth model has necessarily been deeper financial integration with the US.

This is illustrated most vividly by China's holdings of US government bonds (or 'Treasuries'), which ballooned from $60bn in 2000 to over $1trn in 2021. But this actually understates the true extent of financial integration between the US and China. Estimates based on data from the IMF and the Bank for International Settlements suggest that China's financial claims on the US are at least $2.5trn. At the same time, America's financial claims on China are about $400bn.[10]

Moreover, the extent of financial integration between the US- and China-*blocs* is even greater. Based on the country alignments mapped out in Chapter 3, the financial claims of the China-bloc on the US-bloc are something like $9trn, while the US-bloc's claims on the China-bloc are around $6trn.

Financial globalization has therefore gone hand-in-hand with greater financial integration between US- and China-aligned blocs. China's investment in the US and its allies is not just contained to financial securities, such as US Treasuries. Chinese entities have also invested heavily in Western manufacturing and technology firms and have amassed a vast property portfolio across the US and Europe. The Chinese tech giant, Alibaba, provided significant amounts of early-stage funding for the US ride-sharing app, Lyft. And in 2014 the Anbang Insurance Group acquired the Waldorf Astoria Hotel in New York for $1.95 bn, the highest price ever paid for a US hotel at the time. Some of this investment has led to concerns over national security, which I discuss in subsequent chapters.

Investment by the US and its allies in China has been smaller but still significant. This is most evident in joint ventures by firms including Apple and Tesla to build state-of-the-art manufacturing plants in China. But households across the US and Europe have also acquired significant financial assets in China. As of July 2024, well over $10bn was invested in China through US-domiciled mutual funds and exchange-traded funds (ETFs).[11]

With that being said, it is important to keep things in perspective. Despite this inter-bloc integration, the vast bulk of cross-border financial claims lies between US-aligned countries. While the data are patchy, a ballpark estimate is that these now total over $130trn. The cross-border financial claims within the US-bloc are therefore orders of magnitude larger than the claims of China and its allies on the US-bloc. This reflects the fact that cross-border capital flows within the US-bloc dwarf those between the US- and China-blocs. Once again it is difficult to be precise, but I estimate that around four-fifths of all global cross-border flows take place within the US-bloc itself.[12]

To give just one example, it is thought that about $7.5bn of private equity investment flowed between North America and China between 2016 and 2019 – but over the same period more than $65bn of private equity investment flowed between North America and Europe.[13]

Globalization has made the US, China and their respective allies more financially integrated. A sudden rupture in these ties would create havoc in global financial markets with potentially severe economic consequences. But the caricature of China hoovering up vast amounts of assets in the US and Europe obscures the fact that the overwhelming majority of global capital flows take place between the US and its allies, and that the vast bulk of cross-border financial claims remain within the US-bloc.

All of this raises three questions. First, will US–China fracturing accelerate the slowdown in global capital flows that has already taken place over the past decade? Second, as the US and China pull apart, will it spur efforts to unwind the complex web of cross-border financial assets and liabilities that has developed between the two sides over the past four decades? And finally, will fracturing undermine the dollar's central role in the global economy? The remainder of this chapter examines each of these questions in turn.

What drives the global flow of capital?

There are two principal drivers of cross-border capital flows: international trade and international investment decisions. When a country imports a good or service, there is an associated flow of capital in the other direction. The payment for the good or service is made via either a transfer from the importer's bank to the exporter's bank or, more likely, some form of trade finance vehicle. Either way, the transaction results in a flow of capital from the importer to the exporter.

International investment decisions also result in an associated flow of capital across borders. Consider an example in which a US firm builds a factory in China. In this case, there would be a flow of capital from the US to China. From a balance sheet perspective, the external assets of the US would increase or, to put it another way, the US would obtain a financial 'claim' on China – it would have an asset in China which in theory it could liquidate. At the same time, the external liabilities of China would increase.

Overseas investment in factories and the like is a form of what economists call 'foreign direct investment', or FDI. However, the same holds for so-called 'portfolio investment', which involves international purchases of bonds, equities and other securities.

In an interconnected world it is important to distinguish between so-called 'gross' and 'net' capital flows. Suppose a Chinese firm invests $100 in a US firm, which itself invests $75 in China. Gross capital flows represent total capital flows and in this example are $175. Net capital flows represent the balance of overall capital flows and in this example are $25 (i.e. $100 – $75).

Net flows are an important concept because they indicate the extent to which a country is accumulating net external liabilities (or assets). In this example, China's net external assets – or net financial claims on the US – have increased by $25. At the same time, America's net external liabilities have increased by $25.

This is important because a large build-up of net external liabilities leaves a country dependent on maintaining the confidence of foreign investors, and can therefore be extremely destabilizing. Balance of payments and currency crises are nearly always preceded by a significant accumulation of net external liabilities. However, when we are thinking about the future of financial globalization it is the totality of global capital flows that matters – and it is for this reason that we should focus on the implications of fracturing for *gross* capital flows.

Capital flows in a fractured world

One way to think about the effect of fracturing on the value of (gross) capital flows is to consider how it will influence their two key drivers: trade and international investment decisions.

In Chapter 3, I argued that US–China fracturing would not necessarily lead to a substantial reduction in global trade flows. Instead, having grown at rates significantly above that of global GDP in the period of hyper-globalization, it is likely that trade now grows broadly in line with world GDP – meaning that the ratio of trade to world GDP remains roughly flat. If that's the case then capital flows associated with trade transactions will grow at a slower pace than in the globalization age but they won't collapse.

Meanwhile, a relatively contained form of fracturing may have little effect on the overall size of cross-border capital flows relating to international investment decisions. Granted, inter-bloc investment in geopolitically sensitive sectors will slow substantially. This is likely to be particularly true of private equity flows, where rules are less transparent and more vulnerable to political capture, and where positions can be more difficult to exit. But other forms of cross-border investment will increase. If Western firms move the production of strategically important goods and services out of China and into a US ally such as India, Vietnam or Mexico, this will entail significant cross-border investment in order to put the necessary plant, machinery and infrastructure in place.

Instead, it is likely that the overall scale of global capital flows associated with international investment decisions will be influenced primarily by the attitudes of regulators. In this regard, the mood appears to be shifting away from a belief in unfettered capital flows and towards the use of controls to regulate more short-term, speculative flows. This should act as a dampener on overall cross-border capital flows. But this is motivated by a reasonable belief that excessive financial liberalization sowed the seeds of the GFC, and an understandable desire to avoid a repeat of the crisis in future. It has little to do with fracturing.

The net result is that, much like global trade, a contained form of US–China fracturing is unlikely to cause global capital flows to collapse. A more likely outcome is that, having increased at rates significantly above global GDP over the past three decades, they will now grow broadly in line with that of global GDP.

Size versus direction

However, while fracturing is unlikely to have a material effect on the overall size of cross-border capital flows, it will influence the direction of flows. In particular, there is likely to be a shift towards greater intra-bloc flows, and away from inter-bloc flows.

This shift will in part reflect investment required to re-orientate critical supply chains towards more friendly countries. But it will also reflect the fact that Western investors are likely to become more reluctant to invest in China given concerns about potential political interference in certain sectors, sanctions or difficulties in repatriating funds. At the same time, however, it is reasonable to assume that Western investors will try to uphold the wider financial benefits of globalization. The opening up of China provided US investors with access to a fast-growing market as well as an opportunity to diversify portfolios away from traditional markets in America and Europe. These benefits can be retained by investing in other high-growth emerging markets within the US-bloc. While private equity investment in China has slowed, private equity investment in India, for example, has increased five-fold since 2015.[14]

This shift in the direction of cross-border investment flows could have significant macroeconomic effects. US direct investment in China totalled $126bn in 2022. This sounds enormous but must be viewed in the context of China's overall economy. It was in fact equivalent to less than 1 per cent of China's GDP (for 2024). If US investment was to fall to zero, the direct effect on China's economy would be relatively small. However, if this was redirected to an emerging market that aligns more closely with the US, the effects could be significant. $126bn is equivalent to 3 per cent of India's GDP, 6 per cent of Mexico's and more than a quarter of Vietnam's. For these economies, the benefits of capturing even a small slice of the international investment that has previously flowed to China would be significant.[15]

China's surplus will bind it to the US

On the other side of the fracturing divide, Beijing is also reorienting investment flows. This is partly because, in an effort to avoid tariffs and other potential restrictions imposed by Washington, Chinese firms have started to build factories in third-party countries in order to supply the US market. This requires investment.

It is no surprise that this practice is most common in those sectors that form the key fault lines in fracturing. According to the World Bank, in 2023 companies in China invested more than US$11bn in computer manufacturing in other countries, 13 times more than they invested in 2022 and five times more than the annual average in the previous decade.[16] As it happens, this will have the effect of *increasing* inter-bloc flows, since if Chinese firms are to insulate themselves from the consequences of fracturing by locating production in countries allied to America then they will by definition need to invest in plant and facilities in the US-bloc. But these flows are so far relatively small – the $11bn invested in foreign computer manufacturing plants in 2023 is dwarfed by total Chinese overseas investment of $147bn in the same year.[17]

Stepping back, the scale of China's overseas investment is a direct consequence of its structurally high domestic savings rate and persistently large current account surplus. This means it continues to accumulate large amounts of external assets – and it presents Beijing with a growing problem.

There is an increasing awareness among China's leadership of the risks associated with investing in the US and Western economies. This has led to a push to diversify outbound investment. Yet these efforts have encountered two problems. The first is that foreign investment that is made on political rather than economic grounds brings its own set of risks. During the 2010s, China began funnelling its foreign earnings towards overseas investments in a way that aligned with its foreign policy objectives, which were then expanded and formalized with the Belt and Road Initiative. But while the BRI has become a vehicle for diversifying China's outbound investment, it remains one in which decisions over where to lend and on what terms have been made on political as well as economic grounds. The result is that Beijing is now experiencing a rise in default rates in parts of its BRI portfolio. For instance, in 2022, Kenya defaulted on loan repayments for the construction of a high-profile railway linking Nairobi to Mombasa. And China has become embroiled in sovereign default sagas across emerging markets ranging from Zambia to Sri Lanka.

The second problem facing Beijing is more fundamental and is one of size. China's current account surplus has climbed to around $250bn a year and in absence of fundamental economic reform is unlikely to fall over the coming years. There are few economies – and certainly none in the emerging world – that can take on this amount of external liabilities on a sustainable basis. China may seek alternatives to investing in the US: it could, for example, stockpile commodities such as oil or gold. But there are limits to which it could do this. It already holds about 5 per cent of its official reserves in gold, which is relatively high by international standards (most countries hold between 2 per cent and 5 per cent of their official reserves in gold).[18]

It is likely that China will increase its purchases of gold and other precious metals further, and divert more outbound investment to middle-income emerging economies. But the sheer size of its external surplus means that a reasonable share will continue to flow into large and deep Western financial markets.

China's conundrum

Beijing faces a similar conundrum when it comes to what to do with its large *stock* of external financial assets. On the face of it, the fact that China has amassed close to $10trn of overseas assets should give it significant global financial clout. It is the world's major creditor country and, conversely, the US is the world's major debtor nation. But China's large stock of external assets is starting to pose a headache for policymakers in Beijing.

The issue is that a large share of China's external assets is denominated in US dollars. More than 50 per cent of the banking sector's external financial assets are dollar denominated, while dollar assets account for around 60 per cent of China's foreign exchange reserves.[19] And this is a problem for Beijing because it gives the US the ability to sanction or confiscate its assets.

This was not a serious threat in the 1990s and 2000s, when the world was integrating and multilateralism was the order of the day. But this is no longer the case. The US and its allies are increasingly willing to use their financial muscle against their geopolitical adversaries. The most notorious example is the move to freeze $260bn of reserve assets held by Russia following its invasion of Ukraine. But the US has also seized reserve assets held by Afghanistan, as well as imposed financial sanctions on Iran, Venezuela and North Korea that have dramatically curbed each country's ability to transact in international markets.

Perhaps the most troubling aspect of all of this for Beijing is that Moscow had attempted to mitigate the threat of US sanctions by diversifying its reserve assets away from US

The Fractured Age

dollars and towards other currencies, notably euros. But the united front between Europe and the US fatally undermined these efforts. The lesson for Beijing is alarming: in the event of a serious escalation in geopolitical tensions, any asset held in the currency of the US or one of its close allies is potentially subject to seizure.

The challenge in divesting from the dollar

China's problems are compounded by the fact that any attempt to divest its portfolio of dollar-denominated assets would face two significant challenges. The first is that the sheer size of its holdings of dollar-denominated assets prevents them from being unwound quickly – and any attempt to proceed gradually would only undermine the value of China's remaining holdings. A perennial concern is that Beijing will dump its stock of US Treasury bonds. But China is easily the largest foreign holder of Treasuries. A concerted effort to sell a significant part of its portfolio would be visible to banks and brokers across the world. The result would be pain across financial markets and a sell-off in US Treasuries. This would be bad news for the US but also bad news for China since it would reduce the value of its remaining stock of Treasuries. In some ways, therefore, China is a victim of its own success: the sheer scale of the international investment positions it has built up will make them hard to reverse.

The second challenge that China would face is that it would have to find alternative markets capable of absorbing its estimated $10trn of external assets. There is a reason why, when Russia reduced its holdings of dollar reserve assets, it switched to euros: there was nowhere else to go. The purpose of holding reserves is to provide policymakers with a pool of assets they can draw on in the event they encounter balance of payments problems. Accordingly, they must be invested in safe and liquid assets. Investing in exotic financial instruments that swing around in value would undermine the integrity of the country's external balance sheet. In all of this, the currency of denomination is critical. The need for relative stability and liquidity narrows the pool of suitable assets down to those denominated in a handful of currencies.

According to the IMF, more than 85 per cent of reserve assets are denominated in US dollars, euros, Japanese yen, British pounds, Swiss francs and Australian and Canadian dollars. Within this group, the US dollar accounts for 55 per cent of reserves and the euro accounts for just under 20 per cent.[20] Meanwhile, the combined shares accounted for by the yen, Swiss franc, British pound and Australian and Canadian dollars amount to just 10 per cent. In other words, there are a few currencies other than the US dollar in which countries can invest sizeable external assets. What's more, all of the alternatives are currencies of American allies and sit within the US-bloc. China will inevitably try to diversify its external financial assets but roll the clock forward a decade and it is still likely to hold significant assets in US dollars. A major unwinding of the cross-border financial positions that have built up over the past three decades is therefore unlikely.

The true nature of America's exorbitant privilege

This brings us to the question of the role of the dollar within the global financial system. Much of the focus in this regard has been on the dollar's function as the world's primary reserve currency and what former French President (and at the time Finance Minister), Valéry Giscard d'Estaing, termed the 'exorbitant privilege' bestowed on the US government as a result. In fact, the exorbitant privilege that Giscard d'Estaing referred to stemmed from more than just the dollar's function as the world's reserve currency. He was Finance Minister in the 1960s, a period in which the dollar played a central role within the Bretton Woods system of fixed but adjustable exchange rates, which meant that the dollar became the internationally accepted medium of exchange. This created international demand for dollars, which, in the words of Charles de Gaulle, another former French President, enabled the 'United States to be indebted to foreign countries free of charge'.[21]

The dollar's primary role in settling cross-border transactions means that this is as true today as it was in Giscard d'Estaing's time. Close to 90 per cent of all international transactions are settled in US dollars – well in excess of the share of reserves held in dollars and far outweighing America's relative economic size. (The US accounts for about 40 per cent of global GDP at market exchange rates and less than 10 per cent of global exports.) In contrast, only 7 per cent of all global transactions are denominated in renminbi.[22]

This provides significant benefits to the US. First, it creates latent demand for dollars, which, as Giscard d'Estaing suggested and most economists agree, lowers US borrowing costs. Second, the fact that US firms, households and federal and state governments transact internationally in the currency in which they also receive income insulates them from exchange volatility. Finally, and most importantly, in a world of increased geopolitical competition, the widespread use of the dollar extends American influence. It means that the US in effect provides the plumbing for the global financial system. At some point, most cross-border transactions will touch the US banking system, giving Washington a tool with which to keep allies in check and, more importantly, to punish foes.

This has understandably raised alarm in Beijing and has led to a concerted effort by policymakers to create alternative payments systems that cut out the dollar. Central to this is a push to settle trade in renminbi. This has so far been most successful when it comes to trade with very close allies or states subject to US financial sanctions: almost all of China's trade with Russia, Iran and North Korea is denominated in renminbi.

But the push to internationalize the renminbi is widening. In December 2022, a meeting between President Xi Jinping, Mohammed bin Salman and the leaders of the Gulf Cooperation Council (GCC) led to an announcement of what they called a 'new paradigm of all-dimensional energy cooperation', which included a push to settle energy trade between China and the Gulf in renminbi. And during a visit to Beijing in April 2023, Brazilian President Luiz Inácio Lula da Silva called for an end to the dollar's dominance in world trade. It is a good bet that over the next decade the share of global trade settled in renminbi will increase.

The death of the dollar is wildly exaggerated

However, to borrow from Mark Twain, reports of the subsequent death of the dollar were an exaggeration. This is for three reasons.

First, while trade between countries that align with China is growing, it still accounts for only 8 per cent of total global trade. In contrast, over 50 per cent of global trade takes place within the US-bloc, and over 80 per cent of global trade involves a country that aligns with the US. This trade will continue to be denominated overwhelmingly in US dollars.

Second, for the renminbi to become a major international currency, China would need to provide the rest of the world with large quantities of safe, liquid and convertible renminbi-denominated assets to serve as reserves for other central banks and collateral in financial markets. But China's high domestic savings rate means that it will tend to run a large current account surplus, which will make it hard for China to supply significant quantities of renminbi to the rest of the world. China's capital controls also work against the free exchange of renminbi in international markets, which in turn makes foreigners reluctant to hold large quantities of renminbi-denominated assets. A major policy shift would therefore be needed if the renminbi is to seriously challenge the dollar, including reforms to reduce domestic savings and a willingness in Beijing to give up much of the political control over China's economy that is a central feature of the current framework.

Finally, the dollar has several things working in its favour. For a currency to be widely used as an international medium of exchange, it must be readily and cheaply available around the world. That depends on foreigners being willing to hold it in large volumes: in other words, it must function as a store of value.

The dollar is not the only currency that could perform this role. But any alternative would need to share similar attributes: it would have to be backed by strong and stable institutions, and issued by a central bank that operated an open capital account. It is striking that despite the swathe of sanctions and asset freezes imposed on Russia since 2022, around half of its exports are still settled in either dollars or euros.

In addition, any currency that did have these characteristics would have to overcome the strong network effects that underpin the dollar's global dominance. The dollar benefits from what economists call path dependence: its long history as a dominant currency creates an established norm that becomes self-perpetuating. Companies have become accustomed to using the dollar, and shifting to another currency requires overcoming significant inertia and adjustment costs. Financial institutions and payment systems are now optimized for the dollar, making it more convenient for users. And the existence of a wide range of dollar-denominated financial products, covering not just bonds and stocks but also credit and derivatives, reduces transaction costs and reinforces the use of the dollar. All of this creates positive feedback loops that will make the dollar hard to dislodge.

Weaponizing the dollar

The upshot is that, while China will continue to push the use of the renminbi to settle transactions with allies, the US dollar is likely to remain the world's dominant currency for the foreseeable future – and China will struggle to reduce its use of the dollar significantly. This in turn means that America will continue to provide the financial plumbing for much of the global economy. And in a world of heightened geopolitical competition, this will provide Washington with substantial leverage.

Comprehensive financial sanctions have been imposed on Cuba, Iran, North Korea, Syria and, of course, Russia. In addition, targeted financial sanctions have been put in place against individuals and firms that are considered to pose a threat to US national security – including several high-ranking Chinese officials. These sanctions restrict nearly all trade and financial transactions between US firms and individuals, and have become a key tool in America's foreign policy toolkit.

In some cases, so-called 'secondary sanctions' have been imposed. These levy penalties on non-US entities that transact with a government, firm or individual that has been sanctioned by the US. This presents non-US entities with a stark choice: do business with the US or with the sanctioned target. And because the widespread use of the dollar means that most international transactions will at some point touch the US financial system and thus involve a US entity, the choice really boils down to doing business with the sanctioned target or doing business with the rest of the world.

This is, to use a technical term, a 'no brainer' – and it gives the US enormous power. Not only does it provide Washington with a tool to inflict economic and financial pain on its adversaries, it provides a way to ensure that its allies also toe the line. Accordingly, the decision by the US to impose secondary sanctions on Iran (in 2010) and Russia (in 2021) resulted in governments across Europe and the rest of the world replicating US sanctions on both countries.

Secondary sanctions are enormously disruptive for the firms that transact with the sanctioned entity and, since they effectively back America's allies into a corner, they can only be used selectively. But the ability to cut out adversaries from much of the global financial system is a powerful tool in America's arsenal. As fracturing deepens, it will be increasingly difficult for Washington to resist using it.

Financial globalization, with a twist

The upshot is that while fracturing will alter some aspects of financial globalization, it won't reverse it. There is likely to be a shift towards fewer inter-bloc flows in some areas, particularly those deemed to be strategically important or vulnerable to government intervention. But China's persistent current account surplus will mean that it will continue to amass dollar-denominated assets. And the world more generally will remain deeply financially connected with the US dollar at its core. This will be a key source of American strength in a fractured world.

However, in other non-financial areas the US has much less of an advantage over China. This includes some areas of technology, notably green technologies, as well as securing the supplies of critical minerals that will be needed in the economy of the future. In these areas, China has already stolen a march on the US.

CHAPTER 6

Beyond Trade and Finance
The Wider Impact of Fracturing

The economic effects of fracturing will extend well beyond the impact on global trade and financial flows. It will affect some elements of global migration, it will cause governments to direct more effort and resources towards securing supplies of raw materials and it will affect how technologies are developed and then diffused across borders. Over and above this, it will have a broader impact on global economic governance. The period of multilateralism that has dominated since the end of the Cold War is dead. In its place is emerging a more fragmented system of governance, which will make it much harder to rise to the key economic challenges of our times. We must consider each of these factors in order to fully assess the economic consequences of fracturing.

Migration flows in a fractured world

Globalization has historically manifested itself in three ways: cross-border flows of trade, cross-border flows of capital and cross-border flows of people. Migration was a particularly significant part of the wave of globalization experienced in the late nineteenth and early twentieth centuries. But it was also present in the most recent period of globalization. Having held steady at just above 2 per cent between 1960 and 1990, the share of the world's population living outside the country of their birth started to rise in the 1990s and hit 3.6 per cent in 2020. This was the highest figure in the 60 years that the United Nations (UN) had been compiling data.[1]

It is therefore perhaps unsurprising that immigration has become a political minefield across much of the world. A desire to push back against immigration played a critical role in the UK's decision to vote for Brexit in 2016 and the election and re-election of Donald Trump in 2016 and 2024. It has also fuelled the rise of far-right populist parties across Europe, which has been most evident in their strong showing in European parliamentary elections in 2024.

Yet the economic case for immigration remains strong. As Jonathan Portes, a leading economist in the UK, points out, the case for immigration is the logical extension of market economics.[2] In Portes' words:

'If people take decisions on the basis of their own economic self-interest, this will maximize overall welfare. This applies to where people live and work just as much, if not more, than it applies to buying and selling goods and services.'

There are, of course, political limits to what might be an acceptable level of immigration. And the pushback against immigration over the past decade suggests that the US and Europe may be approaching these limits. But most economic studies suggest that immigration has a positive effect on the growth of GDP, and a smaller but still positive effect on the growth of GDP per capita, in destination countries. What's more, these positive effects are likely to become larger over time as domestic populations age. Japan's population is already falling. And forecasts by the United Nations show that in the absence of net migration, Germany, Italy and Korea will each experience a fall in population between now and 2050, while population growth in the US and UK will slow to a crawl. This would have significant consequences for economic growth and the public finances.[3]

As it happens, while the push to restrict immigration seems likely to intensify, it is doubtful that US–China fracturing will play a major role in this. For one thing, most migration takes place between countries within the US- and China-blocs. Of the world's 20 largest migration corridors, only seven involve one China-aligned and one US-aligned country.[4] What's more, some of these – for example migration between Venezuela and Colombia, and Bangladesh and India – are unlikely to be affected by geopolitical rivalry between the US and China.

Instead, to the extent that fracturing has any effect on global people flows, it is more likely to be because governments introduce restrictions on migration in sectors or fields deemed most important for national security. Part of this might include tighter controls on flows of overseas students, particularly in areas that provide access to domestic technology. These migrants are by definition more likely to be skilled, and there are countless empirical studies showing that skilled migrants provide a disproportionate boost to innovation, entrepreneurship and technological progress.

But the numbers involved are likely to be small. To put it into perspective, there were 290,000 Chinese students studying at higher education institutions in the US in 2023.[5] Together, they accounted for less than 2 per cent of all students enrolled in US higher education. Meanwhile, the number of US H1-B visas – the main way in which graduate-level workers in occupations that require specialist skills enter the US – is capped at 85,000 (0.05 per cent of the US workforce). And the H1-B visa programme is also consistently oversubscribed.

It is therefore unlikely that fracturing itself will play a significant role in influencing global migration flows. Instead, the broader effects of fracturing beyond trade and finance are likely to be felt in other ways. Chief among these will be the battle between rival blocs to secure access to critical materials.

Moscow delivers a wake-up call

The COVID-19 pandemic wreaked havoc upon the global economy. As countries locked down, shipments of everything from basic consumer goods to life-saving personal protective equipment ground to a halt. Governments across the world were forced to consider something that most had not needed to for 40 years: supply chain security.

Yet while the pandemic provided a jolt to governments that had grown complacent during the globalization era, from the point of view of fracturing the real wake-up call came 12 months later when Russia invaded Ukraine. As Russian troops poured over the border into eastern

Ukraine, the consensus view was that the US and Europe could hobble Russia's wartime economy by curtailing imports of Russian oil and gas – thus depriving Moscow of much-needed export revenues. In fact, President Putin turned the tables on the West – cutting off flows of Russian natural gas to Europe, and redirecting oil exports to countries in Asia, including India.

The price of energy in European wholesale markets soared, with natural gas prices increasing ten-fold. The pass-through to household energy bills was partly blunted by substantial government subsidies, but this came at the cost of adding extra pressure to fiscal positions that had already weakened significantly in the wake of the pandemic. And while government support cushioned the blow to households it didn't remove it altogether – household utility bills still doubled in some countries, adding fuel to the post-COVID inflation fire that had been raging across Europe.

Europe's energy crisis was not caused by US–China fracturing. But it did provide a stark illustration of the perils of relying on adversaries for supplies of energy and critical minerals in a new era of geopolitical friction. Within the space of two years, Europe's energy map was fundamentally redrawn. Before the war in Ukraine, Russia supplied 40 per cent of the European Union's natural gas and 30 per cent of its oil. By 2023, it supplied just 10 per cent of the region's natural gas and 3 per cent of its oil.[6]

The rapid speed of Europe's energy transformation – while necessary in the circumstances – created significant economic pain. In the four years between 2019 and 2023, the economies of France and the UK grew by just 1.5 per cent, while GDP in Germany flat-lined.[7] By contrast, over the same period the US economy grew by over 8 per cent. The lesson to governments across the world is clear: relying on geopolitical adversaries for supplies of energy and critical materials is fraught with danger and while it is possible to find alternative sources of supply, being forced to do so quickly incurs significant costs. As US–China fracturing intensifies, it is therefore likely that governments on both sides of the divide will take steps to diversify supplies of raw materials and, where possible, source them from friendly countries. The push to secure supplies of key commodities looks set to become a key fault-line in a fractured world.

The fight for commodities in a fractured world

The raw materials and commodities used by modern economies can be divided into four broad groups:

- Energy, including oil, natural gas, coal, and petroleum products.

- Food and agricultural commodities, most notably wheat, corn, soybeans, palm oil and rice.

- Industrial metals, the most important of which are steel (and iron ore which is used in the production of steel), aluminium and bauxite, and copper.

- Minerals needed to support the 'green transition' and technologies of the future. These include lithium, cobalt, nickel, zinc, chromium, platinum, palladium, and rare earth elements.

As fracturing deepens, governments across the world are going to face two challenges. The most immediate will be to prevent the supply of these raw materials from becoming concentrated in one or two countries. Diversification will become the name of the game. The second challenge will be to develop sources of key raw materials from countries within their geopolitical bloc. This will take time and money to develop, as well as a concerted effort at the highest levels of government to court the major producers of these commodities and then keep them onside.

One way of assessing concentration risk – that is to say the extent to which critical commodities are sourced from one or two countries – is to look at the share of global output that is accounted for by the three largest producers of each commodity. This reveals a broad spectrum of risk. At one end, around 90 per cent of the world's production of platinum, palm oil and lithium comes from its three largest producers. At the other, the top three producers account for 35–40 per cent of the global output of oil, petroleum products and copper.[8]

In very general terms, concentration risks are lowest in energy and agricultural commodities. This reflects the fact that these have been essential raw materials for more than 150 years. Governments have poured countless amounts of economic and political capital into bolstering supplies of both energy and food. And viewed through the lens of fracturing, the world's food and energy map looks relatively evenly balanced. Just under half of the world's natural gas is produced in countries that align with China, with a similar share coming from countries that align more closely with the US. The same is true of wheat and corn. Meanwhile, about

40 per cent of the world's oil comes from the China-bloc and 40 per cent comes from the US-bloc.

This is not to say the situation is without risk for either side. A lot depends on whether the major oil producers in the Middle East continue to straddle both blocs. If they break for one side it would have significant adverse consequences for energy security in the other. This is less of a concern for the US, which is now a small net exporter of energy. But it is a major concern for Europe and China. And national security considerations mean that the Middle East remains a region of critical importance to US interests, even though America is now less dependent on imported energy. One thing we can therefore be reasonably confident about is that a fractured world will be one in which Washington, Beijing and Brussels direct considerable effort towards building and strengthening diplomatic relations with the Gulf.

China's grip on critical minerals

However, concentration risks are much greater in the two other broad groups of commodities – industrial metals and minerals needed for the green transition. And in both cases, the map tilts in China's direction.

The fact that China is a dominant player in global industrial metals markets reflects the investment-intensive nature of its growth model, which sucks in vast amounts of materials used in construction. China is the world's largest consumer of copper, iron ore, aluminium, nickel and zinc, and Beijing has understandably taken steps to build ties with major producers.[9] This has shaped its approach to securing supplies of the minerals that will be needed in the green transition and will form core inputs to technologies of the future.

A key part of this strategy has not only been to strengthen ties with major producers but also to invest in and control production in these countries. As Luc Leruth, Adnan Mazarei, Pierre Régibeau and Luc Renneboog note in a working paper produced for the Peterson Institute for International Economics, Chinese influence on the supply chains of key minerals and rare earths 'extends beyond what is commonly assumed ... once one accounts for 'non-transparent webs of ownership and influence'.[10] China has not only strengthened diplomatic ties with key producers in Africa and Latin America, in many cases the actual mining of the commodities themselves is undertaken by Chinese-owned firms or Chinese-funded operations.

The result is that over 80 per cent of the world's cobalt and 70 per cent of the world's rare earths, which are both used extensively in battery technology, are now produced in either China or one of its allies. What's more, focussing just on the extraction of these minerals understates China's dominance. This is because they must be refined in various ways before they are put to use and this is an area in which China is also dominant. For example, while less than 20 per cent of the world's bauxite is extracted in China, nearly 60 per cent of the world's refined aluminium, which is an essential component of everything from solar panels to electricity networks, comes from China. Similarly, about half of the world's refined zinc, which is used extensively in wind and hydro technology, is produced in China. This has given rise to the term 'critical minerals' – a catch-all name for raw materials that are used in new technologies and will be increasingly essential to a country's national security but have a supply chain that is particularly vulnerable to disruption.

America will cultivate new supplies – but at what price?

China has a clear lead over the West when it comes to securing supplies of the critical minerals. The US and its allies have been caught on the back foot and are now playing catch-up. The fact that Europe's energy map has been fundamentally redrawn in the space of just a few years demonstrates that change is possible. Likewise, the fact that the global supply of historically important commodities – energy and food – is relatively evenly distributed across blocs suggests that the same will ultimately happen with the critical minerals that will underpin the economy of the future. However, Washington and its allies are faced with a dilemma. The example of European energy shows that rapid change creates substantial economic disruption and imposes significant costs. But at the same time gradual change means that it will take longer to address vulnerabilities in the supply of critical minerals and therefore will leave economies exposed.

Both the US and Europe are taking steps to develop new sources of supply of critical raw materials, either domestically or in friendly countries. This is partly the result of deliberate efforts by governments to incentivize shifts in supply. For example, the European Union's Critical Minerals Act, passed in 2023, sets targets for minimum shares of EU demand to be covered by domestically-sourced, processed and recycled raw materials.[11] But the market also has an important role to play in this process. As each bloc competes for supplies of critical minerals, their price should rise. The same is true if one country takes steps to cut off supply to another. This in turn should incentivize the exploitation of new sources of supply.

There are several examples from history that illustrate this process in action – most notably the development of oil fields in the North Sea. The fact that these fields lie offshore, deep under the sea bed, made them costly to develop. In the early 1970s, the market price of North Sea oil was broadly similar to the cost of extraction, leaving producers with little profit. But when the oil shock of 1973 sent global oil prices soaring, the economics of North Sea oil suddenly made sense. By the end of the 1970s, the price of North Sea oil was more than double the cost of extraction.[12]

Rare but not scarce

The equivalent in a fractured world may be rare earths. These are the minerals that are critical inputs to a vast number of products from consumer electronics including smartphones and tablets, to green technologies such as wind turbines and solar panels, and military hardware such as F-35 fighter jets.

The most important thing to know about rare earths is that they are not, in fact, rare at all. Indeed, according to the US Geological Survey they are actually 'relatively abundant'. But extracting these minerals is both dirty and expensive.[13] As a result, supply tends to be concentrated in a small number of areas and in countries that have less onerous environmental regulations governing extraction.

For this reason, about 70 per cent of the world's supply of rare earth metals comes from China. And Beijing's grip on the global supply of rare earths provides it with a means to retaliate to US measures against it. As I noted in Chapter 1, when the US in 2023 imposed restrictions on technology exports to China, Beijing responded by cutting the supply of two rare earth minerals: gallium and germanium.

But while China dominates the supply of rare earths, it has only 40 per cent of the world's proven reserves. This is a significant amount, but it means that just under two-thirds of the world's rare earth deposits sit outside China. What's more, these are just the deposits we know about – there are likely to be many more that as yet lie undiscovered. Just as the spike in the oil price in the 1970s led to the exploitation of new sources of oil, including in the North Sea, so any attempts to curtail the supply of rare earths is likely to cause a price spike that makes it profitable to mine new sources.

With that said, the path ahead for the US and its allies is unlikely to be smooth or easy. For a start, any interruption in supply can still cause significant damage in terms of lost output. There are implications for inflation too. One concern is that the fight for commodities will contribute to higher inflation in the West – after all, it is likely that in many areas higher prices will be required to incentivize new production. But this gets the economics wrong. Higher prices may be likely in the short term – either because demand for scarce resources increases, or supplies are constrained by geopolitical adversaries. But as I've just argued, this should incentivize new supply or the development of technologies that reduce demand for these minerals, which in turn should lead to a fall in prices. In other words, supply shortages and price spikes will eventually be followed by supply gluts and price falls. Geopolitical competition is therefore likely to mean more *volatile* rates of inflation rather than *higher* rates of inflation. As we shall see in Chapter 7, this will complicate life for the world's major central banks.

Technological leadership in a fractured world

So China has a clear lead over the US when it comes to securing critical minerals in a fractured world. What about the tussle to become the world's technological leader?

The image of China as the 'workshop to the world' bears little resemblance to the Chinese economy of today. Granted, China remains the world's largest producer of most basic consumer goods, from toys and furniture to flat-screen televisions. But in many areas it now also pushes the global technological frontier. China now issues more patents each year than any other country; it leads the US in several critical technologies, including batteries and advanced telecoms networks; and the Chinese Academy of Sciences is the largest research organization in the world. In this sense, its economy is a strange hybrid of low-end manufacturing powerhouse and global technological leader.

China's technological prowess is the result of several decades of deliberate and focussed industrial policy. Beijing's objectives in this regard were laid bare in the 'Made in China 2025' plan, which has formed the cornerstone of industrial strategy since it was unveiled in 2015. It has the twin objectives of transforming China into a global leader in high-tech industries, while at the same time reducing its dependence on foreign technologies. Consistent with this, China's latest Five Year Plan, which was announced in 2021, contains ambitions to boost research in everything from AI and semiconductors to biotechnology and regenerative medicine.

The state has marshalled its considerable resources to meet these goals. Much of this has gone through China's university system, and has placed a heavy emphasis on experimental research into new technologies and their application. According to the OECD, while the US outspends China three-to-one on basic research, China now outspends the US (and every other country) in experimental research.[14]

China leads in green tech

It is this focus on experimentation and application that has transformed China into a global leader in several areas. This is particularly true of green technology. Notably, China is now the dominant global force in battery technology, which in turn has allowed it to develop strength in related areas such as electric vehicles. China's control over the supplies of the raw materials that are critical inputs across broad swathes of green technologies reinforces its dominant position.

This has brought benefits to the rest of the world. Applying China's low-cost, high-productivity manufacturing sector to climate technology has transformed the economics of the green transition. For example, the cost of solar energy has fallen by more than one-third since 2019 as Chinese production has surged.[15]

But it also brings challenges. There are growing concerns in Washington, Brussels and London that the substantial subsidies provided to Chinese manufacturers by Beijing have created an uneven playing field that will hinder the development of domestic production in critical green technologies of the future. These concerns relate in part to jobs. As green tech grows in importance, firms in these sectors will become substantial employers. But a bigger concern surrounds national security and the wisdom of becoming excessively dependent on a geopolitical rival for what are clearly going to become critical technologies of the future.

America plays catch-up

The US and its allies have already taken steps to cut out Chinese components, including those manufactured by telecoms giants Huawei and ZTE, from domestic 5G networks. As it happens, Australia was the first country to sense the threat in this area. It instituted a ban on Huawei and ZTE from domestic telecoms infrastructure in 2018.[16] At the time, the move was controversial but it has since been followed by similar decisions in the US, UK, France, Italy and – eventually – Germany, which has set out steps to remove Chinese components from its domestic 5G network by 2029. The shift in attitudes towards Chinese telecoms firms is likely to be repeated in other critical technologies. And it is a good bet that the next battle will take place over batteries and electric vehicles.

There are two concerns in this area: energy security and data and privacy issues. The idea that renewables will inevitably replace oil as the energy source of the future is a hackneyed one. In fact, while the International Energy Agency (IEA) projects that global oil demand will peak by the end of this decade, it still expects that by 2040 just over 20 per cent of the world's energy needs will be met by oil. At the same time, however, it is clear that renewable sources of energy are going to become increasingly important. The IEA projects that by 2040 just under 40 per cent of global energy demand will be met by renewables.[17] And just as there was a push by governments in the twentieth century to build alliances with major oil producers in order to secure energy supplies, the same will be true of renewables and associated green technologies in this century. For the West, this will necessitate taking steps to reduce (and perhaps eliminate) dependence on Chinese battery technology.

Meanwhile, concerns over data and privacy are reflected in the fact that US policymakers now routinely talk about 'connected vehicles' rather than electric vehicles. These are vehicles with internet connectivity and communication technologies that enable the exchange of data with other vehicles and external systems. This technology underpins many of the features that are now common in modern-day vehicles, from real-time traffic updates and navigation systems to remote diagnostics. It makes our vehicles both safer and more efficient. But it is also the stuff of nightmares for officials responsible for upholding national security. Not only could a large-scale attack on connected vehicles wreak havoc on transportation networks but they also entail the transfer of data on an industrial scale that could be hacked by foreign adversaries. Having Chinese components embedded deep within these networks creates obvious vulnerabilities.

Accordingly, the US has taken an increasingly aggressive approach to both cutting out Chinese technology and promoting the development of domestic production across these areas. The 2022 Inflation Reduction Act contained $369bn in subsidies to support the development of domestic production of electric vehicles and 'clean tech' products, including batteries and renewable energy. At the same time the US has levied punitive tariffs of up to 100 per cent on imports of electric vehicles, solar panels and battery components from China. Advisers to President Trump have repeatedly made clear the central importance of constraining China's capabilities in critically important areas of technology. The objective is clear – level the playing field for domestic US producers and cut out Chinese technology.

Europe will seek a middle ground

Governments in Europe have taken a more cautious approach to cutting ties with Chinese green tech. It is sometimes argued that this is because Europe lacks the fiscal firepower to subsidize the expansion of its green industries to the same extent that the US has. But the real issue is one of political coordination and prioritization.

A package of green subsidies that is similar in size to that contained within America's IRA would be equivalent to less than 2 per cent of European Union GDP, and the costs would be spread over several years. It is difficult to believe that Europe's bond markets would have trouble absorbing government debt issuance on this scale – not least because it would be used to finance an expansion of Europe's capital stock, and therefore would pay dividends in terms of future growth.

But Europe has struggled to muster a unified response. The most effective way to finance a large package of green subsidies would be through the issuance of bonds that are jointly backed by all EU governments – this, after all, is a collective challenge faced by all nations. But this approach would be fiercely resisted by the region's fiscally stronger countries, most notably Germany.

At the same time, governments in Europe face a different set of trade-offs to the US when it comes to cutting ties with China. These are partly economic – China is the largest export market outside of Europe for Germany. But it also reflects a growing appreciation within European capitals that the region's green tech sector is woefully underdeveloped and that governments are unlikely to meet net zero targets if they cut out Chinese technology altogether. These targets generally have much greater political currency in Europe than in the US, and thus present a dilemma for policymakers.

Taken together this suggests Europe will adopt a much less aggressive approach to Chinese green technology. As is often the case, governments in the region are likely to seek a middle ground – accepting the need to import batteries and electric vehicles from China, while at the same time investing in capacity both domestically and in other friendly countries. It's possible that this approach will succeed. Europe has a long tradition of muddling through, and very often it works. But it is a strategy that risks trapping

Europe between two adversaries: dependent on China for supplies of critical green technologies and increasingly vulnerable to US pressure to cut ties.

Technological leadership through the lens of blocs

China may have developed into a global tech leader in many areas, including green technology, but America still holds several important cards. For a start, its economic heft allows it to pour vast sums of money into developing new technologies. According to the most recent data from the OECD, America still spends close to 15 per cent more than China on overall research and development when adjusted for the domestic purchasing power of their respective currencies.[18]

America is also home to the world's leading science and technology research institutes. According to the QS World University Rankings, five of the top ten colleges for engineering and technology are in the US.[19] What's more, its colleges are deeply integrated within the fabric of the country's technological ecosystem, meaning that innovations are quickly commercialized and diffused throughout the economy. As a result, many of the world's breakthrough technologies of the past decade have come from the US. This includes the new breed of large language models that are at the forefront of the artificial intelligence revolution. Key AI breakthroughs, including the development of ChatGPT (by OpenAI) and BERT (by Google), have originated from US entities, cementing America's position as the global leader in this field.

Crucially, from the perspective of fracturing, we need to think about technological leadership through the lens of US- and China-aligned blocs. This tips the scales in America's favour. The US may be home to five of the top ten universities for engineering and technology, but *all* of the top 10 and 17 of the top 20 are in countries that align more naturally with the US. In contrast, just one of the world's top 20 engineering and technology colleges sits within the China-bloc (Tsinghua in Beijing was placed 11 in the 2024 QS rankings). Similarly, while China just edges the US in the 'Nature Index' – an index produced by the publisher of the same name that counts contributions to leading scientific journals – institutions from within the US-bloc have three times the number of citations of those in the China-bloc.[20]

This may all seem academic (in both senses of the word) but it has important implications in the real world. The COVID-19 pandemic provided a real-life test of scientific capabilities in different economies, with the key measure of success being the speed with which countries could produce safe and effective vaccines to protect against the virus. In the event, firms from the US and China (along with the UK) all registered vaccines with the regulatory authorities in their respective jurisdictions at the same time in December 2020 – a remarkable feat in the circumstances.

However, the real breakthrough in the race to develop vaccines was the application of so-called mRNA technology, which was pioneered through a partnership between Pfizer (a US firm) and BioNTech (a German firm). This new technology produced a vaccine that was both more effective and faster to administer. The speed with which mRNA vaccines were developed and brought to market would not have been possible without the collaboration of scientists, firms and governments in different countries – and the fact it happened in the US-bloc speaks to its enduring strength in key areas of technology.

Chip leadership will be key

The race to develop COVID-19 vaccines provided a real-life test of the scientific capabilities of both blocs, but the real battle for technological leadership will come in other areas, particularly semiconductors. These are components so tiny that they are measured in fractions of millimetres, but they form the backbone of the modern digital economy. Chips control everything from smartphones and cars to advanced healthcare and military equipment. Without them, the technology that we rely on each day would cease to function. Indeed, it is no exaggeration to say that they have become so fundamental to the functioning of our economies that advances in chip making will play a critical role in determining the speed of overall technological development. Accordingly, there is a good chance that technological leadership in a fractured world will belong to the country – or bloc – that leads in semiconductors. This is an area that is dominated by the US and its allies.

Semiconductor firms typically organize their activities around the two main stages of production: design and manufacturing. Because chips are made or 'fabricated', companies that focus on chip design are known as 'fabless firms'. Meanwhile, companies that focus on chip production are known as 'foundries'. Both are underpinned by a complex web of semiconductor technology, a critical component of which are lithography machines. These print intricate patterns onto silicon wafers, creating the tiny circuits that form the core of semiconductor devices.

The world's leading chip designers include Qualcomm, a US firm known for its Snapdragon processors that are used in many high-end smartphones, and Nvidia, also a US firm, renowned for its graphics processing units that are used in AI hardware. The world's leading chip manufacturers are TSMC (Taiwan) and Samsung (Korea), which between them account for 75 per cent of the global semiconductor market – with TSMC alone accounting for 60 per cent.[21] The world's leading producers of lithography machines are ASML (from the Netherlands) and Tokyo Electron (from Japan).

All of these firms sit within the US-bloc – and it is a chokehold over China that policymakers in Washington are squeezing increasingly tight. In October 2022, the US banned the export of its most advanced chips, as well as the tools to produce them, to China. But it has also successfully pressured its allies to curb exports of chips and chip technology to China. TSMC has stopped exporting some of its most advanced chips used in AI and quantum computing to China. Meanwhile, in 2024 ASML announced that it would stop providing service support for its most advanced DUV lithography machines (used to produce cutting-edge chips) in China – in effect curtailing their lifespan.

In response, Beijing has redoubled efforts to replace foreign suppliers of semiconductors and semiconductor technology. According to the US Department of Commerce,

China's government provided $150bn in subsidies to domestic chip producers.[22] As a result, China's domestic semiconductor supply chain is deepening and its capabilities are increasing with surprising speed.

Progress in semiconductor technology is measured in the size of chips that are produced. This determines the performance, cost and efficiency of the chip – and the smaller it is, the better. In 2023, Huawei shocked the world – and especially China hawks in Washington – when it launched a smartphone that used 7 nanometer (nm) chips produced by China's leading semiconductor firm, SMIC. China's chip industry is shrouded in secrecy but most experts had assumed that it was several years away from being able to produce 7nm semiconductors. It is now thought that SMIC may be on the cusp of producing a 5nm chip.[23]

Even so, China's chip industry remains some distance from the cutting edge. 5nm chips are now routinely used in everyday technology – for example, Apple started to use them in iPhones in 2022. Meanwhile, Samsung and TSMC are now producing 3nm chips. These advanced chips are already being used to power the latest generation of smartphones and laptops as well as large language models and advanced military equipment. What's more, as technology develops, their use will become increasingly common until they are replaced by even more powerful chips – it is thought that 1nm chips will be in commercial use as soon as 2027.[24]

America's advantage

China's progress in developing a domestic chip industry has been rapid, but it remains some way from matching the world's most advanced semiconductor technology. What's more, the progress it has made so far has been aided in part by technology that has been imported or replicated. China is likely to find that its access to foreign technology is increasingly restricted, meaning it will need to forge its own path from here. The scale of the challenge is formidable. Not only do the US and its allies hold a sizeable lead in this area but they are outspending China in order to maintain this advantage. In 2023, capital expenditure by TSMC alone was four times that of SMIC.

The key question for the US is whether it can keep its allies onside and continue to restrict the flow of advanced semiconductor technology to China. If it can, most observers believe that while China will make further progress in this area, it will continue to lag the US by 5–10 years.[25] And if the US-bloc can retain the lead in foundational technologies such as semiconductors, the chances are that it will remain the technological leader in a fractured world.

Global economic governance in a fractured world

The push to secure supplies of critical minerals and restrict access to advanced technologies is an example of how fracturing will affect policy at a national level. But it will also have a profound effect on policy making at a global level. This is the final area we need to consider in order to form a fuller picture of the economic impact of fracturing.

The global institutions that have underpinned the international 'rules-based system' for the past 40 years are to varying extents already either defunct or losing influence. The World Trade Organization lies in a state of paralysis. The World Bank has been challenged by the emergence of national and regional development banks, including the Asian Development Bank, the Asian Infrastructure Investment Bank (based in Beijing), the Inter-American Development Bank (focussed on Latin America) and the African Development Bank. And the IMF has found itself caught between performing its traditional role as a lender of last resort to countries facing balance of payments crises, and the seemingly more attractive proposition of becoming a sort of global economic think-tank capable of dispensing policy advice on everything from education policy to climate objectives.

It is easy to cast blame on politicians for neglecting the multilateral institutions that have supported 40 years of peace and prosperity. America carries much of the blame. The decision by the US to block appointments to the WTO court was nakedly political. Washington has also resisted efforts to give large emerging economies, particularly China, a greater share of voting rights on the IMF's board. Such a move would make the institution more representative of the global economy that it is supposed to serve.

But the reality is that these institutions are relics. This partly reflects economic developments over the past four decades. When the IMF was conceived in the aftermath of the Second World War, its primary function was to provide financing to countries experiencing balance of payments crises. However, the rise of China and other creditor nations, notably Saudi Arabia and the Gulf states, has provided an alternative to IMF financing. The combined external assets of China and the Gulf Cooperation Council of countries amount to more than $11trn – more than 15 times larger than the total assets of the IMF.[26]

Political objectives have shifted too. Multilateral institutions such as the IMF and World Bank were created to foster economic, financial and political integration between countries. But the deepening geopolitical rivalry between the US and China means that barriers are now purposefully being erected in many areas.

It is likely that the US will need to rely on a mix of subsidies and tariffs if it is to build a green tech industry that can compete with China's. Similarly, China will have to continue dolling out huge subsidies to its domestic chip industry if it is to close the gap between itself and the US and its allies. These policies and practices violate the principles that the institutions of the international rules-based system were built to uphold. But the harsh truth is that in a world of geopolitical rivalry, the rules-based approach to global economic governance is no longer compatible with the priorities of governments in some areas. Countries – and blocs – are acting out of self-interest. Cooperation is being replaced by competition.

The IMF, World Bank, WTO and others will continue to try to promote liberal, rules-based values. This is a laudable aim. But the global economy is evolving in ways that have undermined – and will continue to undermine – their influence.

The rise of bilateral lending removes an anchor for reform

Countless PhD theses will be written on the political and geopolitical implications of the declining influence of multilateral institutions.[27] But there are two immediate economic consequences that we must consider: one that affects individual countries and another that affects global economic governance more generally.

For individual countries, the rise of bilateral lending, in place of multilateral lending by bodies such as the IMF, has important consequences. The IMF has in the past been criticized – not unreasonably – for imposing excessively strict conditions on borrowers. This has included the need for severe fiscal austerity, which, while necessary in order to put both the public finances and balance of payments of borrowers on a more sustainable footing, has sometimes been imposed without consideration of the broader socio-economic effects.

To be fair to the IMF, lessons have been learnt and the conditions attached to recent programmes have been more moderate. But it is also the case that the IMF and other multilateral institutions have become convenient scapegoats for politicians (and some commentators) that refuse to accept economic realities. Nations that turn to the IMF have, by definition, been living beyond their means. Accordingly, some squeeze on domestic demand is almost always going to be necessary in order to put the economy on a more stable footing. What's more, criticizing the IMF ignores the fact that programmes have frequently acted as an anchor for reform in these countries. This was the case, for example, in Korea in the late-1990s and Turkey in the early-2000s. As a result, in addition to providing immediate financial assistance, IMF programmes have helped lay the groundwork for macro stability and improved economic performance over the medium term.

Bilateral lending comes with no such conditions attached. Indeed, it is often dispensed according to political rather than economic objectives. Accordingly, it brings none of the benefits of acting as an anchor for economic reform in borrower countries. What's more, partly because funding has been provided on political rather than economic grounds, some countries are now struggling to repay their debts. China has become embroiled in difficult debt renegotiations in countries ranging from Zambia and Ethiopia to Sri Lanka. In each case, the lack of an official resolution framework has complicated debt restructuring, lengthening the process and deepening economic pain. The consequences of all of this will fall more heavily on the world's poorest.

Crisis management in a fractured world

The second consequence relates to global economic governance more fundamentally. One concern that is often voiced in disregard is that the decline of multilateral institutions will make it much harder to coordinate policy responses to economic crises. But while this may be true at the margins, it is unlikely to be a major constraint that many seem to believe.

A lot is made of the coordinated cuts to interest rates by the world's major central banks at the height of the Global Financial Crisis in October 2008. But the key point is that countries were really acting out of self-interest – demand was collapsing and central banks were loosening policy anyway.

That is not to say that lines of communication between the world's major central banks and finance ministries are not important in times of crisis. On the contrary, they are critical to maintaining a real-time flow of information between policymakers and responding quickly and appropriately. For example, in the wake of the collapse of Lehman Brothers in 2007 and at the outbreak of the COVID-19 pandemic, a collapse in counterparty confidence meant that access to foreign currency funding markets froze. In both cases, the rapid establishment of currency swap lines between the Fed and other major central banks helped to maintain foreign currency funding and repair market functioning.

But lines of communication between the world's major central banks are unlikely to be severed by US–China fracturing, not least because most of them sit within the US-bloc. Moreover, the optimal policy response at a global level during an economic crisis also tends to be the same as the optimal response at a national level: there typically is a common need to support demand and maintain market functioning. Accordingly, fracturing is unlikely to be a significant impediment to an effective policy response in times of global economic crises.

Collective actions problems get harder to solve

Instead, the biggest challenges will come in areas where the problems are less acute and where the incentives facing individual governments do not align with the collective interest. The development of vaccines during the COVID-19 pandemic is a good example. As we saw earlier, the race to develop vaccines involved some exchange of technology and intellectual property within the US-bloc. But this aside, governments across the world fell victim to vaccine nationalism – prioritizing the rollout of jabs to domestic populations rather than those most in need at a global level.

This approach to policymaking is likely to become more common in a fractured world. Governments have always prioritized their own interests over those of others – they are, after all, accountable to their own citizens. But this will be even more the case as fracturing deepens and multilateralism declines. What's more, to the extent that wider interests are taken into account, this is likely to be coordinated through groups of 'like-minded' countries rather than through truly global institutions like the IMF, WTO or United Nations.

On one side, this includes the G7 group of advanced economies, NATO, and various security groups including Five Eyes (the US, UK, Canada, Australia and New Zealand) and the Quad (the US, Japan, India and Australia). On the other, it includes the Shanghai Cooperation Organisation (made up, among others, of China, Russia, India and several countries in Central Asia) and the BRICs. In each case, these groups form around the interests and values of their main sponsors – the US and China. The result is a growing bifurcation of policy coordination at a global level. And it means that in a fractured world it will become increasingly difficult to solve problems that require collective action.

The climate challenge gets tougher

The greatest collective action problem of our times is addressing climate change. In what was perhaps the final great multilateral agreement of the globalization era, signatories to the 'Paris Agreement', which was finalized at the COP21 summit in France in 2015, committed to keep the global average temperature rise this century to no more than 2 degrees centigrade above pre-industrial levels, and ideally to no more than 1.5 degrees centigrade above pre-industrial levels. In order to achieve this, they agreed to reduce their net carbon emissions to zero by 2050.

The Paris Agreement itself is supposedly legally binding but there is no official enforcement mechanism. Instead, countries set what are called 'nationally defined contributions' towards meeting the Paris targets and are required to publish plans setting out how they intend to meet them. On the current trajectory most are set to fall well short of their targets.

Stepping back from the politics around climate change, two things must happen in order for countries to achieve net zero carbon emissions by 2050. The first is that there must be a substantial shift in energy investment away from fossil fuels and towards renewables. In 2023, about one-third of energy investment went into fossil fuels and two-thirds went into renewables. The IEA thinks investment in renewables will need to increase to around 90 per cent of total energy investment by the end of this decade and then stay there over the next 20 years if the world is to achieve net zero by 2050.

The second thing that must happen in order to achieve net zero is that countries will need either to forgo economic activity in some carbon-intensive areas or find new, greener, ways of continuing these activities. This includes energy-intensive forms of transport, notably aviation, and energy-intensive industrial processes, including the production of steel and cement.

Yet because carbon emissions are by their nature global, there is an inherent incentive for countries to free ride on the actions of others. Switching from carbon-intensive to carbon-neutral forms of economic activity naturally incurs costs, but the benefits of lower carbon emissions globally are felt by all. Each country therefore has an incentive to delay action, relying on other countries to bear the costs of transition while at the same time benefiting from their actions. But because the same incentives apply to every country then little (or no) action is taken at all. Indeed, several countries – notably the major oil and gas producers – have an incentive to delay the green transition altogether. It is striking that the US – which is now the world's largest oil producer – has adopted a more pro-fossil fuel position during a second Trump administration.*

In this sense actions to reduce carbon emissions, and to address climate change more broadly, must be collectivized. This requires organization and coordination across the world's major economies. It needs a comprehensive and consistent policy framework covering incentives, regulation and financing for developing economies. And there must be a credible enforcement mechanism, which punishes slippage and rewards over-achievement. This proved fiendishly difficult to achieve in the era of global cooperation. Achieving it in a world of geo-economic competition and declining multilateralism will be even harder.

---

*In January 2025, President Trump announced his intention to withdraw the US from the Paris Agreement.

Most countries will continue to make progress towards net zero targets, not least because pressure from some parts of the electorate – notably the current generation of younger voters – is likely to grow. But progress will be slower than might otherwise be the case if there was an effective global push towards meeting these targets. It will take decades for the macroeconomic consequences of all of this to be fully felt. Most economists agree that the biggest costs will come over the second half of this century. This is a vastly complicated issue that lies outside the parameters of this book. But when the costs are felt, they will come to bear on the world's poorest – particularly those sub-Saharan Africa and low-lying countries in South Asia. And in the meantime, extreme weather events will become more frequent, disrupting harvests, whipsawing food prices, and adding to the list of reasons to expect global inflation to become more volatile.

The fractured world

So where does this leave us? I have shown how US–China fracturing will shape international flows of trade, capital and technology; how it will lead to a concerted effort by governments to secure supplies of critical minerals from friendly countries; and how it will have a profound effect on global economic governance. But what impact will all of this have on economic growth and prosperity? It is to this question that we now turn.

CHAPTER 7

Growth and Prosperity in a Fractured World

In Chapters 4, 5 and 6, I set out what are likely to be the key economic consequences of US–China fracturing. I discussed how fracturing might affect global trade, capital and labour flows, how it will influence technological development, how it will shape efforts to secure supplies of raw materials, and the implications for global economic governance. In this chapter, I assess what all of this means for growth and prosperity on both sides of the fracturing divide.

One important point to make clear from the outset is that fracturing is a process that is evolving. The fault lines along which the US and China are pulling apart are becoming clear, but the exact form this will take is not yet settled. There are several ways in which a more extreme form of fracturing could develop, including a retreat into broader isolationism by the US or outright military conflict between the two blocs, which would have severe consequences for economic growth. These are considered in Chapter 8.

All of this makes it difficult to pin down exactly what one's 'base case' should be when thinking about how the structure of the global economy will change over the next decade or so. But there are still reasons to think that the split that both sides will pursue will be a partial one. Trade and capital are still flowing between the US and China, even if they are doing so at a slower pace than in the globalization era. This should therefore be the basis on which we construct a central view of the implications for growth and prosperity. With this in mind, here is the story so far:

- The emergence of China as a strategic competitor to the US is causing the world's two largest economies to pull apart. Most countries would prefer not to pick a side but over time it is increasingly likely that they will be forced to do so.

- The result is that the world is fracturing into two blocs – one that aligns with the US and another that aligns with China. The edges around each bloc will be fuzzy and will shift over time. But the split is unlikely to be even. The US-bloc is likely to be both larger and more economically diverse than the China-bloc.

- Fracturing is not the same as deglobalization. The re-election of Donald Trump has raised the risk of a global trade war, but this is not bound to happen – not least because support for broad trade protection in other major economies is still limited. Viewed over the long run, Western governments are most likely to take steps to decouple trade in areas that compromise national security, supply chain security, or global technological leadership. A large share of global trade will therefore continue despite fracturing. And a major reshoring of production to the US and Europe is unlikely.

- Similarly, while global capital flows will slow, they are unlikely to collapse. Flows from the US-bloc to the China-bloc are likely to slow. But China's large current account surplus means that it will continue to invest large sums in the US-bloc.

- This reflects the enduring dominance of the US financial markets and the dollar. While China will push its allies to transact in renminbi, this is unlikely to seriously challenge the dollar's position as the world's major currency. The US will continue to provide the financial plumbing for the global economy. This will provide Washington with a powerful tool to coerce allies and punish adversaries.

- China has an edge over the US when it comes to securing supplies of raw materials and will remain a global leader in some areas, including green technology. But the US is likely to retain a broader technological lead over China, in part due to the technological strength of its allies.

- Finally, multilateralism is on the wane. This will make it harder to solve challenges that require collective action.

Globalization, the West and the need for a sense of perspective

So how will fracturing affect future prosperity? Global integration boosts output by breaking down barriers between economies. This expands the global market for goods and services and enables countries to specialize in areas of production in which they have a comparative advantage. This in turn leads to both greater competition and a more efficient allocation of resources. Accordingly, anything that causes integration to reverse is likely to weigh on global economic growth.

With that said, when it comes to the consequences for growth in Western economies, some perspective is required. While most studies find a positive link between increased economic integration and GDP growth, it is difficult to argue that globalization has had a large positive effect on growth in the US and Europe over the past three decades. Indeed, productivity growth in the G7 economies has slowed during this period. Growth in output per worker averaged 1.5 per cent a year in the 1990s, 1.0 per cent in the 2000s and just under 1 per cent a year in the 2010s.[1]

Of course, this slowdown in productivity growth has nothing to do with globalization. Rather, it reflects a combination of other factors, of which a critically important one has been the effects of the 2007–08 Global Financial Crisis. This caused a collapse in output during the crisis, which was then followed by only a tepid recovery as the need to repair the balance sheets of banks and households weighed on aggregate demand. The COVID-19 pandemic subsequently caused economic activity to crater in 2020, albeit with a much swifter recovery in 2021–22. But this simply underlines the point that the effect that globalization had on economic growth in the West was small and easily overwhelmed by other factors. While globalization has reshaped the world, it has not been the primary determinant of economic growth in the US or Europe over the past 40 years.

Diversity matters

What's more, US–China fracturing will not reverse all the economic gains created by globalization in the West. Only a fraction of global trade and capital flows will be affected.

The movement of some high-skilled workers from the China-bloc to the US-bloc will slow, but this is a small part of over-all migration flows. And the dollar is unlikely to be dislodged from its position at the heart of the global economy.

More fundamentally, the US holds a critical advantage over China when it comes to managing the challenges posed by fracturing: the economic diversity of its allies. The US-bloc is made up of four broad groups of economies:

- High-end manufacturers and other technological leaders, including Japan, Germany, Taiwan and Korea.

- Global leaders in services, including the UK.

- Emerging market manufacturers and other low-cost economies, including India, Mexico, Vietnam, the Philippines and Poland.

- Commodity producers, including Canada, Australia, New Zealand and Colombia.

Added to this, the US itself is a world leader in high-end manufacturing, technology and services, as well as a major energy producer. Diversity matters because it means that blocs are better able to replicate the global economy as a whole and, as a result, continue to benefit from the economics of comparative advantage. So in instances where concerns over national security or supply chain vulnerabilities mean that production is shifted out of China and into the US-bloc, it can be moved to another economy with low wage costs and an existing manufacturing base, such as

Vietnam or Mexico. This would retain the core benefits of comparative advantage and prevent a significant increase in firms' costs, thereby limiting any pass-through to higher inflation in advanced economies.

Parsing the costs

This is not to say that any such move would be costless. There are two reasons why firms in the US-bloc are likely to reconfigure supply chains over the next decade. The first is that the wrenching experience of the pandemic followed by the war in Ukraine has revealed the potential costs of having single points of failure within supply chains. This is causing corporate leaders across the world to reassess the conventional wisdom of the past 40 years, which has been to construct the leanest and most efficient supply chains possible, and means there is now an increased focus in boardrooms on building resilience. This could happen in various ways – firms could diversify supply chains, so that the same components are sourced from different suppliers, or they could hold more inventory as insurance against shocks further down supply chains. Both would incur a cost.

The second reason why firms may reconfigure supply chains is that, as fracturing deepens, they will be pushed to do so by governments. Indeed, this is already happening. In a conference call with investors in 2022, Wendell Huang, the chief financial officer of Taiwanese chip giant TSMC, stated bluntly that the firm's decision to build a semiconductor fab in Arizona was 'based on customers' requests'.[2] In this instance, the customer was Apple, and Apple made the request in order to support a push by the US government to develop a domestic semiconductor industry, which itself was motivated by concerns around supply chain security and preserving America's technological leadership. TSMC has remained tight-lipped about the costs involved, but in the same conference call it did divulge that 'the initial costs of overseas fabs are higher than our fabs in Taiwan' and that the construction costs alone were 'four-to-five times greater for a US fab versus a fab in Taiwan'.

A matter of speed and scale

So reconfiguring supply chains incurs costs. But these costs are easier for companies to bear if the changes are phased in gradually. Toyota is credited with having pioneered the concept of lean manufacturing in the 1980s. But the company has adopted a new approach in recent years as it has been forced to face the vulnerabilities inherent within ultra-efficient supply chains. A huge earthquake and tsunami that hit Japan in 2011 forced the firm to close its domestic operations for nearly two months. This led to a collapse in Toyota's production in Japan itself, but a shortage of locally produced parts also hit output at its plants elsewhere in the world. For several weeks, Toyota's factories in North America operated at 30 per cent capacity.[3]

In response, Toyota shifted its approach, regionalizing parts of its supply chain and forcing single-source suppliers to either hold more inventory or disperse production. This transformed Toyota's supply chain and increased business resilience.[4] But the costs of doing so were manageable, in part because the changes were phased in over time and spread over several years. This contrasted with the shift in Europe's energy supply in the wake of Russia's invasion of Ukraine, which happened rapidly and imposed substantial costs on households, firms and governments.

Accordingly, while it is common to assume that any attempt to reconfigure supply chains – either to decouple from China or to increase resilience more generally – will necessarily lead to greater inefficiencies, and therefore higher costs and prices, this is not always the case. Indeed, according to the academics Sunil Chopra and ManMohan Sodhi, 'for large companies in particular, building [supply chain] resilience is often relatively inexpensive, and in many cases it can be done without increasing costs'.[5] The critical factor is the conditions under which any changes are made. If shifts in supply chains happen gradually and affect only a small part of overall trade, then the associated economic dislocation is likely to be smaller than many now assume.

Benefits for some

What's more, it's likely that a contained form of fracturing would bring benefits to smaller emerging economies that can position themselves as reliable allies of the US and therefore attract production that is relocated from China for strategic reasons. The economies that have been most successful at doing this so far have been Vietnam and Mexico. Neither will become another China in terms of global dominance of industry or exports. Their populations are a fraction of the size of China's and, in Mexico's case, there are significant governance and security issues that will remain a headwind to economic development.

But they each have advantages – beyond their political alignment with America – that have enabled them to position themselves as an alternative location for manufacturers and to gain market share in the US. Vietnam is home to a large number of well-educated workers, particularly engineers, which, coupled with its location, has enabled it to integrate within the vast global supply chains for consumer electronics that run through Asia. Mexico benefits from its proximity to markets in the US and Canada. Both have comparatively low labour costs. Put all of this together and it is no surprise that both Mexico and Vietnam have experienced a surge in exports to the US since 2018.

India is another potential winner from fracturing. It is the one country with China's scale – in 2023 it overtook China to become the world's most populous nation. And while long thought of as a services-driven economy, high levels of investment are starting to help to develop a vibrant manufacturing sector. Apple has started to build iPhones in India – about 15 per cent of the company's iPhones are made there now – and is now exporting from its plants there. Other parts of the supply chain are likely to follow.

None of these countries will challenge China's dominance across a broad range of manufacturing. But they will carve out areas of specialism and become increasingly important suppliers to the US market. If any economies are to benefit from fracturing, it will be them.

AI to the rescue?

For the US and other advanced economies in the West, the key point to keep in mind is that while globalization had a positive effect on GDP growth, the effect was generally small and ultimately overwhelmed by other factors. The productivity gains associated with the computer and ICT revolution were the principal drivers of a pick-up in US GDP growth in the 1990s. Conversely, the bursting of credit and housing bubbles and the associated damage to balance sheets were the primary reasons for the collapse in economic output in 2008 and its subsequent slow recovery over the following decade. A gradual and contained fracturing of the global economy, along the lines described at the start of this chapter, is likely to have a similar but opposite effect to that of globalization: it will weigh on growth in advanced economies, but the drag is likely to be modest and outweighed by other forces.

One such force could come from the artificial intelligence revolution. The economic consequences of AI are unclear and the source of great disagreement among economists. At the heart of the debate is the question of whether AI constitutes what is known as a 'general purpose technology', or GPT. These are technologies that have a wide range of applications across different sectors of the economy and have historically been the source of significant improvements in productivity. The three classic examples of GPTs are steam power, electricity and information technology, including desktop computing and the internet. All three led to substantial increases in productivity, albeit over very different timeframes – the diffusion of steam power throughout economies took several decades, whereas the main impact of the ICT revolution happened over a short period in the 1990s.

The mention of artificial intelligence conjures up images of self-driving cars and robot servants. But the real breakthrough in AI over the past five years has been the development of large language models. These are models capable of processing vast amounts of data and generating original text, images, audio and video. (For this reason they are known as 'generative AI'.) The foundational LLMs have been models such as OpenAI's ChatGPT and Google's Bard (now called Gemini). But because of Moore's Law – which is generally taken to mean that computer processing power doubles roughly every two years – these models are advancing at an extremely rapid pace. The power of an LLM can be measured by the number of parameters that the model adjusts during training to improve its performance. Chat GPT-3, which was released in 2020, is said to contain 175 billion parameters; Chat GPT-4, which was released three years later, is rumoured to contain 1.7 trillion parameters. And models will only get more powerful. Within a few years we will have LLMs that perform like Chat GPT-4 on steroids.

When it comes to what this means for economic growth, the key issues are how widely AI can be applied and whether it can be considered a general purpose technology. Generative AI, and in particular LLMs, has the potential to revolutionize how cognitive tasks are performed by knowledge workers mainly, but not exclusively, in the service sector. This revolution has already started in the software industry and is spreading to other areas like education, translation services, supply chain management, legal and accounting services, copywriting, design and illustration and medical diagnostics. Meanwhile, other forms of AI will continue to develop. This includes everything from driverless cars and advanced robotics to drone delivery.

Based on this, there are reasonable grounds to believe that AI should be considered a general purpose technology – and that it will transform productivity growth in advanced economies within the US-bloc.[6] Economists at both Goldman Sachs and Capital Economics have independently concluded that AI could increase productivity growth in the US by around 1.0–1.5 per cent a year in the decade after its widespread adoption.[7] If the boost from AI is only a fraction of this amount, it will more than offset any drag from a contained form of fracturing.

Inflation more volatile, not higher

How will fracturing affect inflation? There is a growing view among economists at investment banks and fund managers that the end of globalization is another reason to believe that advanced economies have entered a new era of higher inflation.[8] But while it's likely that inflation will be higher over the next decade than it has been over the past one, this has more to do with the fading of the deflationary forces created by the Global Financial Crisis than it does with globalization.

Once again, some perspective is required. Most studies suggest that although globalization contributed to a drop in global inflation, the effect was relatively small. Reasonable estimates suggest that globalization may have shaved up to 1 percentage point off annual inflation in advanced economies between the mid-1980s and mid-2000s.[9] But this was dwarfed by the overall fall in inflation in these economies during this period. Inflation in the G7 economies fell from 12.4 per cent in 1980 to 4.4 per cent in 1990, 2.1 per cent in 2000 and 1.4 per cent in 2010.[10] The main cause of this decline was institutional change: independent central banks that pursued inflation targets, and labour market reforms that suppressed the power of unions and wage bargainers. The effects of the 2008 Global Financial Crisis then added to deflationary pressures at the start of the 2010s. Globalization helped to bring down inflation in advanced economies, but it was not the principal reason for its fall.

Moreover, as I have argued throughout this book, fracturing does not mean that globalization is going into reverse. Where the location of production of goods and services shifts, it is likely to move to another low-cost centre in a country that is more geopolitically aligned. The ambition of populist politicians in Western economies to engineer a great reshoring of manufacturing is likely to go unfulfilled. Meanwhile, the effect on immigration – and therefore labour supply – is likely to be small.

Accordingly, I think it is wrong to believe that fracturing will itself lead to a substantially higher rate of average inflation in advanced economies within the US-bloc. Instead, inflation is likely to become more volatile.

Globalization had the effect of expanding aggregate supply at the global level. Fracturing won't destroy global supply, but it will cause it to become more fragmented in the sectors most affected. If supply in these areas is cut off for a time, then prices of the affected goods or services will surge, putting upward pressure on inflation. However, once new supplies are established, prices will come down. And because inflation measures the rate of change in prices, the effect could even be to create *deflation* in the affected areas.

Imagine for example that, motivated by the national security concerns around the 'Internet of Things' I discussed in Chapter 4, Washington imposes a ban on the use of Chinese-produced Wi-Fi modules in consumer goods sold in the US. This would cut off the supply of these modules and disrupt the production of all manner of 'smart' goods that are connected to the internet, from smart doorbells and lightbulbs to smart watches. The result would be an increase in the price charged to consumers.

But the ban would also incentivize the production of Wi-Fi modules in other low-cost countries that align more closely to the US. Over time, this would increase supply and leave producers of the smart goods for which they are critical component parts with a choice – either keep the price of the final goods unchanged at their new, higher level and pad their margins (in which case consumer price inflation for these items will fall to zero) or pass the reduction in costs onto consumers (in which case there will be consumer price deflation in these areas).

Central banks must double down on inflation targets

This is a highly stylized example, but it illustrates how fracturing will cause shocks that create supply shortages that may then be followed by supply gluts. This has important implications for the conduct of monetary policy. The models that central banks use to forecast inflation tend to focus on short-term shifts in demand and assume that the supply side of the economy grows at a steady long-term pace. In a fractured world, central banks need to update their thinking to include greater consideration of supply-side developments.

The correct policy response to the example I described would be to 'look through' the supply shock and leave monetary policy settings unchanged. Tightening policy in response to the initial jump in prices would not only cause an unnecessary squeeze on demand, and thus over-all economic activity, but it could also threaten the subsequent response in supply – since higher prices play a role in incentivizing new sources of production. Yet doing so requires that central banks correctly identify the nature of the supply shock and have a clear analytical framework for thinking about them in their models.

It also requires that they keep so-called 'inflation expectations' anchored throughout the period of the supply shock. Milton Friedman is best remembered as the economist who pioneered the theory of monetarism, which – incorrectly, as it turned out – argued that controlling the money supply was key to controlling inflation. Among Friedman's most important theoretical contributions was the central importance that inflation expectations play in determining actual inflation. This is because expectations of future inflation affect wage- and price-setting behaviour, and thus become self-fulfilling. If workers believe that inflation is going to be higher next year than it is this year, they will bargain for higher wages. This in turn will boost their spending power and thus aggregate demand, which will then lead to a rise in prices – meaning that the belief of higher future inflation becomes a reality.

This is important in the context of central banks' ability to 'look through' inflation shocks caused by supply-side disruptions of the type I described earlier. If firms and workers believe that the rise in inflation will persist, then they will adjust their behaviour, thus causing second-round effects on wages and prices that will ensure that the rise in inflation is indeed long lasting. As a result, central banks would have to tighten policy in order to bring inflation back to target. The key to avoiding this is to ensure that inflation expectations are well anchored. This requires the central bank to be able to articulate the cause of the price shock, and to convince the households and businesses that it is temporary. The credibility of its inflation targeting framework becomes paramount.

What does this mean in practice? Clearly it requires that central banks are successful in keeping inflation at or close to target most of the time. But it also requires that central banks make clear that their primary objective is maintaining price stability. Over the past decade there have been various calls to expand the remit of central banks to cover everything from contributing to the green transition to helping to raise productivity growth. Meanwhile, in August 2020 the Fed reformed its policy framework, moving away from a fixed inflation target to one that targeted the average rate of inflation over an unspecified period.[11]

While these changes and suggestions were made with the best of intentions, they risk sending the message that policymakers have gone soft on their core task of keeping price inflation low and stable. This in turn risks causing inflation expectations to become unanchored and, in a world more prone to supply shocks, increases the risk that spikes in inflation that would otherwise be temporary become longer-lasting. The implications for central banks are clear: a fractured world should be one in which they double down on sticking to inflation targets.

The upshot is that, all other things being equal, a contained form of fracturing is likely to exert a drag on economic growth in the US and other advanced economies in its bloc, but one that is small and overwhelmed by other factors. Meanwhile, it is unlikely to cause a sharp rise in inflation but could cause inflation to become more volatile. What about the consequences for China?

China has more to lose from shifting supply chains

China was the biggest winner in the globalization era, and so has more to lose now that it has ended. As I argued in Chapter 4, it is far more reliant on the US as a source of demand than it is on allies within the China-bloc. This is reflected in its large bilateral trade surplus with the US, which totalled $400bn in 2022, as well as its bilateral surpluses with other US allies including the euro-zone and Japan.[12]

It goes without saying that this leaves it extremely vulnerable to any attempt by the US and its allies to cut imports from China on a large scale. But as I have argued, any such move is unlikely. Fracturing is being driven by a growing geopolitical rivalry between the US and China, and there are few geopolitical reasons to cut imports of most consumer goods from China. Large amounts of inter-bloc trade will therefore be unaffected by fracturing. Instead, efforts by the US and its allies to limit trade ties with China will focus primarily on areas that threaten national security, supply chain security and technological leadership. This is likely to include:

- semiconductors;

- smart goods (i.e. those connected to the internet);

- telecoms infrastructure;

- some areas of green technology, including batteries and electric vehicles;

- quantum computing;

- critical minerals; and

- pharmaceuticals.

These areas together account for 15–20 per cent of China's exports to the US-bloc, equivalent to 3–4 per cent of its GDP.[13] This represents the share of China's economy that is potentially vulnerable to a reconfiguration of supply chains caused by fracturing. But it is unlikely that all trade in these areas will be disrupted – I have argued, for example, that Europe is likely to continue importing significant amounts of green technology from China. What's more, the change that does happen is likely to be spread over several years. Accordingly, changes to supply chains caused by fracturing are unlikely to have a meaningful effect on economic growth in China from one quarter to the next.

Productivity holds the key

Shifts in patterns of trade affect the demand for goods and services. But economic growth over the long term is governed by developments on the supply side of economies. This is because while demand fluctuates over the cycle and affects resource utilization, without improvements in an economy's ability to produce goods and services it cannot grow beyond its current limits.

A country's economic output over the long run is therefore determined by the number of workers it has and the amount they produce, or their 'productivity'. The latter is the really crucial ingredient. Indeed, as the Nobel Prize-winning economist Paul Krugman put it, 'productivity isn't everything, but, in the long run, it is almost everything'.[14]

Productivity – or output per worker – is influenced by myriad factors, from the size of a country's capital stock to the education of its workforce. Viewed through this lens, fracturing will pose two challenges to China's economy. The first relates to technological progress, and the second relates to the broader approach to resource allocation across the economy.

America's strength is China's weakness

If one of America's key strengths is the economic diversity of its bloc, then one of China's great weaknesses is the lack of variety within its bloc. This is a particular issue when it comes to sustaining technological progress, which is the lifeblood of productivity growth. As I have argued, China holds an advantage over the US in several areas of technology, including green tech. But the US and its allies hold the advantage in cutting-edge foundational technologies, most notably semiconductors and software. These technologies are 'foundational' in the sense that they have a broad range of applications. As such, they regulate the pace of technological progress more generally. And the fact that they are designed and produced in the US-bloc means that Washington has a chokehold over Beijing: by restricting the flow of cutting-edge foundational technology to China, the US can slow its pace of technological progress.

This is why diversity matters. Because China's bloc is dominated by China itself and otherwise made up of smaller emerging economies and commodity producers, it has few alternative suppliers of the hi-tech inputs that it currently sources from the West and which are now the subject of export bans. Instead, China will need to develop these capabilities itself. It is likely to succeed in this regard but it will take time and lots of money. In his book, *Chip War*, Chris Miller argues that it will take up to a decade and cost well over $1trn for China to build an all-domestic supply chain to produce chips that rival the cutting-edge semiconductors currently manufactured by the likes of TSMC and Samsung.[15]

These estimates are, of course, highly uncertain. But the point is that this will consume substantial resources that could have been deployed more productively if China was able to rely on imports of semiconductors from the West. More fundamentally, China's drive towards self-sufficiency in these areas will reinforce an old model of growth that has been spectacularly successful but is now reaching its limits.

Hitting the buffers

China's economic development over the past four decades has been underpinned by an extremely high level of domestic savings which various arms of the state – from the central government to state-owned banks and state-owned enterprises – have then channelled into high levels of investment. Investment has accounted for an average of over 40 per cent of GDP over the past decade.[16] This result has been an enormous upgrading of China's capital stock.

Compared to the size of its population, China's capital stock is now 70 per cent larger than those of Korea and Japan when they were at a similar stage of development, and three times the size of Taiwan's when it was at a similar stage of development.[17] What this means in practice is that China is now home to the world's largest container port (Shanghai), the world's longest high-speed rail network, and the world's largest hydroelectric power station (the Three Gorges Dam). This is the infrastructure that has underpinned its rise to become the world's largest manufacturer.

However, the counterpart to China's high level of domestic savings is a low level of consumer spending. Household consumption accounts for about 40 per cent of GDP compared with about 70 per cent of GDP in the US. This has meant that China has become reliant on exports and investment as a source of demand. This has significant consequences. For a start, it is difficult for the world's second largest economy to rely on exports as a significant source of demand. China's sheer size means that if it continues to run large trade surpluses it will inevitably be drawn into conflict with other major economies, as we are now seeing.

Meanwhile, investing close to half of GDP is difficult at the best of times, but particularly when China's capital stock is now relatively advanced for its level of development and the state is playing an even greater role in determining the allocation of resources. This makes generating returns on investment extremely difficult.

One way to think about this is to look at China's incremental capital-output ratio or ICOR, a measure of how much investment is needed to generate an additional unit of GDP. China's ICOR has soared in recent years as investment has become increasingly inefficient. In 2008, it stood at around three – meaning that three units of investment produced one unit of GDP. But China's ICOR has now risen to almost nine, meaning that the economy requires nine units of investment to produce one unit of GDP. Yet while investment is becoming more inefficient, it continues to account for over 40 per cent of GDP. The counterpart to this is a drop in productivity growth which is pulling down long-run potential growth.

Doubling down

The key to reinvigorating China's growth over the long term lies in reforms to lower the domestic savings rate and rebalance the sources of demand away from investment and exports and towards household consumption. On the supply side, the centre needs to relinquish control and let the market do more of the work in terms of allocating resources, both capital and labour. China's government recognizes this. As far back as 2007, then-Chinese Premier Wen Jiabao declared that the country's economic growth trajectory was 'unstable, unbalanced, uncoordinated and unsustainable'.[18] But implementing the reforms necessary to shift paths has proven to be difficult. Fracturing will make it much harder.

Beijing has responded to the threat posed by fracturing by making a push for self-sufficiency. High-level documents and speeches by China's leaders routinely reference the need to accelerate the development of the country's technological base and improve self-reliance.[19] This is not unreasonable. After all, if there is a risk that America and its allies might seek to sever ties with China in key areas then it is sensible to build domestic capabilities and resilience. But doing so necessarily involves greater investment. And it also requires that any such investment is directed by the state.

This has manifested itself in several ways, from the targets for self-sufficiency set as part of the Made in China 2025 programme to the soft loans issued by state-owned banks to help achieve them. But the result is the same: fracturing is causing China's leadership to double down on a growth model that they themselves recognize has reached its limits.

Heading to 2 per cent

Accordingly, the policy response to fracturing is adding to the headwinds that are already facing China's economy. In addition to slowing productivity, China is facing a demographic time bomb as the effects of the 'One Child Policy', which was officially scrapped in 2016, start to bite. Over the next decade, the United Nations estimates that China's working-age population is set to fall by around 0.5 per cent a year. There are currently around 970 million people of working-age in China but the UN thinks this will have dropped to 860 million by 2040. This stands in stark contrast to peer competitors elsewhere in the emerging world such as India, where the working-age population is forecast to grow by nearly 10 per cent over the next decade.[20]

Piecing this together, I believe that China's economy is heading for a structural and sustained slowdown in growth over the coming years – and that fracturing will add to this slowdown. By 2030 it is not difficult to imagine that China's potential rate of GDP growth could have slowed to as little as 2 per cent a year.

This would represent a radical departure from the rates of expansion that turbo-charged China's development over the past several decades. GDP growth averaged over 10 per cent a year in the 2000s and in excess of 7.5 per cent a year in the 2010s.[21] Over the coming decade, the economy will grow at a fraction of these rates. That will have significant consequences. It will mean that Chinese households will have to become accustomed to a slower rate of income growth, and Chinese firms will have to accept a lower rate of profit growth. It will also bring all manner of social and political pressures that the government will need to find a way of managing.

What's more, with trend growth in the US also running at around 2.0–2.5 per cent it would mean that the economies of both America and China would be growing at similar rates. This would radically reframe the narrative around fracturing. China would no longer be an economic juggernaut that will inevitably challenge American hegemony. Instead, it would mean that both the US and China were global superpowers but that *both* were contending with much slower rates of economic growth than had been the norm at the start of the globalization era. This risks creating a situation in which each side blames the other for their perceived economic troubles – and that fracturing evolves in a way that produces significantly worse outcomes for the US, China and the rest of the world.

CHAPTER 8

Deeper Splits, Warring Blocs

The economic costs of a relatively contained form of fracturing would be manageable for the US-bloc but more significant for China. Yet the exact form that fracturing will take is still unclear. At one end of the spectrum, it is possible that the forces that are driving fracturing will start to dissipate. But at the other end, there are various forms of fracturing that would impose significantly greater economic costs on both sides. The path we ultimately end up on will be determined by four things: whether China changes course and reforms; whether fracturing can be contained to sensitive areas; whether the US remains a leader that the rest of the West coalesces around; and whether the two come into conflict. These questions raise the possibility of a different future. In this chapter I assess each in turn.

Could China change course?

There is nothing inevitable about fracturing. History shows that large economies can coexist peacefully. But in order to do so they must share a common set of values. This was the case, for example, with the US and the UK in the late nineteenth and early twentieth centuries. Accordingly, in order for the forces driving fracturing to dissipate, China would need to change course and pivot towards democracy and liberalism.

It is extremely doubtful that this will happen under the current leadership. But President Xi is now into his seventies. Nature may intervene and force a change in leadership in China. This would create a vacuum at the top. It is extremely uncertain how it would be filled.

History provides some grounds for optimism. After all, the last leader to consolidate power on the same scale as Xi was Mao and after Mao's death in 1976, China embarked on a programme of economic liberalization under Deng Xiaoping. The shift under Deng was motivated in part by the need to reinvigorate a moribund economy. And as I set out in the previous chapter, any leader that came to power in China in the coming years would also inherit an economy in need of reform. It is possible that, just as Mao was followed by Deng, Xi will be followed by a new generation of leaders that push for renewed reform and greater liberalization, which in turn would quell the forces of fracturing.

But the parallels with the transition from Mao to Deng only go so far. Whereas Mao's Cultural Revolution was driven by ideological fervour and Deng's reforms by pragmatism, Xi's leadership has been marked by a focus on control and national rejuvenation. By dismantling the norms of collective leadership that emerged after Deng, Xi has entrenched his personal authority at every level of government. The removal of presidential term limits and the elimination of rival factions suggest that even after Xi's departure his influence will remain embedded within the structure of the Communist Party. One plausible future is that Xi's hand-picked successors simply continue his policies, ensuring the party retains its tight grip on power, much as it did under Mao, albeit without the ideological chaos of the Maoist years.

The social dynamics within China are also different from the Deng era. After Mao's death, Deng was able to ease the country's harshest political controls without endangering the party's monopoly on power. Today, the Party's social contract – economic growth in exchange for political obedience – is fraying, but Xi's surveillance apparatus and repression have kept dissent in check. Without widespread organized opposition, the likelihood of significant social reform is slim. Any discontent is likely to be managed with the same tools of censorship, surveillance and selective repression used by Xi.

Finally, China's position in the world has also shifted. Under Deng, China pursued a policy of 'hiding one's strength, biding one's time', avoiding direct confrontation while focusing on internal growth. That growth has transformed China into the world's second largest economy and means it no longer has to bide its time. Xi has reversed Deng's approach, projecting Chinese power abroad through assertive diplomacy and military modernization. After Xi, China's foreign policy may continue on this assertive path, with national pride and competition with the West driving its actions. Future leaders may refine or recalibrate this approach, but China's push for regional and global influence will persist.

This being the case, those hoping that the post-Xi era will bring a wave of liberalizing reforms that might open the way to warmer relations with the US may find themselves disappointed. The path ahead is more likely to reflect Xi's centralization of power, his deep suspicion of political liberalization and his pursuit of national rejuvenation – all of which will sustain China's geopolitical rivalry with the US.

A broader split

As things stand right now, if the relatively contained form of fracturing that I have outlined in earlier chapters fails to emerge it is therefore likely to be because a harder rather than softer split develops between the two blocs. One way this could happen is if what has so far been a relatively limited form of fracturing evolves into a much broader split covering many more areas. In this scenario, the fissure between the US- and China-blocs would not just be contained to areas of strategic importance – it would widen to include trade in basic consumer goods, a greater number of commodities and raw materials, and services including education, health and tourism. Capital flows between blocs could also be dramatically reduced, and inter-bloc holdings of financial assets could be unwound. Restrictions on transfers of technology would not just be limited to the cutting-edge, they would include many 'lagging'-edge products.

It goes without saying that the wider the fracture in the global economy, the greater the economic disruption and cost. This would be felt in a number of ways. Firms that export to rival blocs would see their markets shrink, which in turn would squeeze their revenues and the wages paid to workers. At the same time, consumers who purchase goods and services from rival blocs would face higher prices. Domestic firms would respond by producing competing versions of the same products. But it would be costly to do this across the broad spectrum of goods and services that are currently traded between blocs. These costs would get passed on to consumers. Similarly, firms that import component parts from rival blocs would also face higher costs when sourcing domestic substitutes. Some of this cost would get absorbed in margins, but some would get passed on to consumers.

The net result of all of this would be a substantial hit to real incomes and real GDP. What's more, there would also be negative consequences beyond those revealed in the economic statistics. Notably, consumers in both blocs would be faced with less choice and, in some cases, inferior products.

In 2023, economists at the IMF published a paper that attempted to quantify the effects of a broader fragmentation of the global economy.[1] It assumed that the world would split into US- and China-aligned blocs and that all trade between the blocs would be prohibited. The authors arrived at three conclusions.

First, the economic costs of such a split would be enormous and at least as large as those caused by the Global Financial Crisis of 2008. Second, the speed at which this fracture occurred would be critical to determining its eventual costs. If it occurred in a relatively gradual manner, the paper argued, there would be a permanent reduction in global GDP of around 2.5 per cent. But if the split happened rapidly then the adjustment in supply chains would have to occur more quickly and the associated costs would increase.

Under these circumstances the authors concluded that there would be a permanent hit to global GDP of around 7 per cent. (For context, most studies suggest that the Global Financial Crisis led to a permanent reduction in global GDP of 2–4 per cent.)

Finally, the authors found that the costs would be substantially greater for lower-income economies. This would be because they are heavily dependent on imports and exports of basic products, including commodities, for which it is more costly to find new suppliers. In their 'gradual' fracturing scenario, the authors found that advanced economies would face a permanent reduction in GDP of just under 2.5 per cent but low-income countries would face a permanent reduction in output of more than 4 per cent. An economic hit of this size would greatly increase the risks of debt crises and exacerbate social instability and food insecurity in low-income countries. A broader fracturing between the US and China would create large losses for all, but these would fall disproportionately on the shoulders of the world's poor.

In search of a motive

Of course, attaching precise numbers to the costs created by these shifts is fraught with difficulty. It relies on models that often struggle to fully capture the interdependencies and reflexivities within economic systems. It is also possible to quibble with some of the IMF's assumptions. For example, the authors assume that it is the strength of trade ties alone that will determine whether a country aligns with the US or China. Yet as I argue in Chapter 3, the reality is more complicated. But there is a bigger question hanging over all of this, which is: what would cause a wider split between blocs to emerge?

Fracturing is being driven by geopolitics and, in this context, issues around national security and technological leadership are something that bind countries within blocs together. It is unclear whether it would be possible to get widespread support for a broader break between blocs. To name just one example, the strength of its commercial ties with China means that Germany would fiercely resist efforts to restrict trade and technology transfers in areas beyond those deemed absolutely essential for national security reasons. The same is likely to be true of other US allies with strong trade relationships with China, including Japan, Korea and Australia.

It is likely that the 'yard' within the 'small yard, high fence' characterization of fracturing will widen over time. Technological development means that products that are deemed cutting edge and strategically important today will eventually become commonplace. This will naturally tend to widen the scope of fracturing. But if the scope of fracturing widens such that it leads to a dramatic reduction in trade or capital flows then it is likely to be because countries start to pursue their own, more aggressive, agenda. By its nature this would be uncoordinated and represent an individual rather than collective split. This brings us to the question of how cohesive blocs really are.

A third or fourth bloc?

The reason why the economic costs of fracturing are likely to be lower for the US than they are for China is that America benefits from a larger and economically more diverse set of allies. This will allow it to retain many of the benefits of globalization but also sever ties with China in sensitive areas.

But this is not bound to happen. It is possible that a cohesive bloc does not form around America, in which case the economic costs for the US-bloc would be greater. One way in which this could happen is if the other major economies in the US-bloc – notably Europe, but also large emerging markets including India – attempted to form separate blocs under their own leadership. If this were to happen, the world would splinter into several blocs, with each trying to outdo the other. The result would be greater fragmentation on the supply side of the global economy and substantially higher economic costs.

There are several periods in history in which there have been more than two rival global economic superpowers. In the sixteenth and seventeenth centuries, European colonial powers each controlled different parts of the global economy: Spain dominated Latin America, Portugal controlled trade routes to Asia and parts of Africa and Brazil, the Netherlands became a major trading and financial centre with a strong presence in South-East Asia, and the UK and France each developed colonies in North America, the Caribbean and Africa. The UK also controlled India, which became known as the 'Jewel in the Crown' of the British Empire. But substantial amounts of trade also took place between these supposedly rival blocs. This was a period in which, for the most part, the dominant global powers pushed integration, not fragmentation.

Governments will rightly defend their own interests, but the reality is that it is difficult to see any other major economy rivalling either the US or China in terms of geo-economic heft. In particular, the degree to which the US exerts economic, financial, technological and military control will make it hard for other countries within its bloc to break out and forge a radically different path. Europe is the only region within the US-bloc with the potential to rival America but a lack of political integration – and thus the ability to speak with one voice – will continue to prevent it from doing so. French President Emmanuel Macron's vision of 'strategic autonomy' for Europe has so far amounted to little more than a few soundbites. In every major geopolitical decision – from sanctions on Russia and Iran to restrictions on Huawei and other leading Chinese tech firms – Europe has followed America's lead. Relations between the major powers within the US-bloc will ebb and flow, but the evidence so far is that when push comes to shove, America's allies are likely to fall into line.

America could cede its advantage

A more likely way in which a cohesive bloc fails to form around the US is that, rather than other economies successfully forging their own path, America itself adopts a more isolationist approach and cuts ties with both China *and* the rest of the world. Indeed, the re-election of Donald Trump on an avowedly nationalist platform has significantly increased the odds of such a shift occurring.

Admittedly, we have been here before. During the first Trump administration tariffs became a tool of economic policy and were threatened regularly and enacted occasionally in order to defend US interests. But despite

Trump's fiery rhetoric, the actions his administration took against America's traditional allies were fairly modest. The North American Free Trade Agreement with Mexico and Canada was reformed rather than axed altogether. Its successor – the US–Mexico–Canada–Agreement, or USMCA – tightened labour and environmental standards to the benefit of US producers, and contained several provisions to support US-based automakers. But trade between the US and Mexico has continued to flourish, in part because manufacturers have moved production to Mexico in order to escape more punitive tariffs on US imports from China. In 2023, Mexico's goods exports to the US hit a record high of over $470bn.[2]

Similarly, in 2018 the Trump administration levied tariffs on $6.4bn of imports of steel and aluminium from the European Union. The official grounds for the move was that it would defend US national security interests, but in truth it was a thinly veiled attempt to support US steel and metal workers that formed part of Trump's base within blue-collar manufacturing. Yet these tariffs covered only 2 per cent of US imports from the EU and did not stop US trade with Europe – or indeed the EU's trade surplus with America – from increasing during Trump's term in office.[3]

It's possible that Trump's bark once again proves to be worse than his bite. Threats to levy universal tariffs on all US imports could simply be a bargaining chip that eventually gets traded away in return for promises from other governments to purchase more US exports or increase contributions to joint defence budgets.

But it requires a leap of faith to believe that this will be the case. What's more, the platform on which Trump was re-elected was more radical in both tone and substance than that on which he was first elected in 2016. With this in mind, and given the direction of travel over the past decade, it is no longer impossible to imagine that the US could make a more serious push towards isolationism.

The economic costs of isolationism

A shift towards isolationism could take many forms. A pullback in US support for Ukraine – or indeed for other nations that rely on America for security guarantees – would represent a form of military isolationism. This would have echoes of the 'America First' movement that advocated a non-interventionist stance towards the Second World War and was supported, among others, by pioneering aviator Charles Lindbergh. A move towards greater military isolationism by the US today would have long-term economic repercussions, not least because, in the absence of the 'world's policeman', it is likely that the global economy would become more prone to shocks. As Russia's invasion of Ukraine illustrated, military shocks can have significant economic consequences that extend well beyond the zone of conflict. Even so, the costs associated with a shift towards military isolationism by the US would be indirect and difficult to anticipate. In contrast, the costs associated with a shift towards greater *economic* isolationism would be more immediate and easier to identify.

The programme on which Donald Trump won re-election in 2024 contained clues as to what a more isolationist economic agenda might look like. For a start, it would almost certainly involve much higher tariffs on US imports. One misconception that is frequently repeated by Trump and his supporters is that the costs of tariffs are borne by countries that export to the US. This is wrong. Tariffs are paid by importers and are a tax on the consumption of imported products. Accordingly, the costs are borne by consumers. The impact on consumer spending and aggregate demand could be blunted if the government then used the revenue raised by tariffs to either increase public spending or cut taxes. But in the short term there would still be an increase in consumer prices. And over the long run, very high tariffs would damage America's long-term potential growth rate, since they would reduce productivity growth in the tradable sector and hamper the transfer of technology and know-how.

It is also likely that a more isolationist agenda would entail stricter limits on immigration. The Congressional Budget Office estimates that just over 80 per cent of the increase in the adult population in the US since 2022 has been due to net migration, with close to two-thirds coming from unauthorized immigrants.[4] A more isolationist shift would be likely to entail measures to significantly reduce legal immigration and eliminate unauthorized immigration entirely. It could also include the widespread extradition of undocumented immigrants. The economic effects of any such policy would be enormous. According to the Department of Homeland Security there were 11 million undocumented migrants in the US in 2022.[5] It is thought that about two-thirds of this number may be active in the US labour market.

If the US government successfully implemented a plan to remove all undocumented workers it would therefore reduce America's workforce by around 4 per cent. At the same time, measures to clamp down on legal immigration and eradicate illegal immigration would reduce the future growth of the labour force by around 0.5–0.75 percentage points a year. And while the squeeze in the labour supply would result in higher wages for domestic workers this would be more than offset by a rise in prices in response to weaker supply.

Taken together, such extreme policies on trade and immigration, combined with the broader consequences of a shift towards isolationism, such as the impact on business confidence, could plausibly knock about 4–5 per cent off of US GDP at the outset and then reduce the economy's potential growth rate from about 3.0 per cent a year to less than 2.0 per cent a year. Wind the clock forward a decade and it is not inconceivable that the US economy might be 10–15 per cent smaller than would be the case in the absence of these policies – and that China would be on course to overtake it to become the world's largest economy.

America first means America last

In practice, an isolationist shift by the US could vary enormously in both its focus and severity. Even so, any step towards greater isolationism would diminish America's strategic influence in the world. It would no longer be able to prevail upon its allies based on a shared sense of values. This would have practical implications. The success of US restrictions on exports of advanced semiconductor technology to China has relied upon Washington being able to bring pressure to bear on key producers in allied countries, such as ASML, the Netherlands-based producer of lithography machines. This has sometimes required the cooperation of friendly governments, which would be much harder to achieve if the US could not draw upon a common set of shared values. A more isolationist US would also create an opportunity for China to pick off US allies and pull them into its bloc. It is difficult to be precise about the costs of an isolationist shift by the US because it would depend on what form it took and how far it went. But the two things we can be reasonably sure about are that it would make the US worse off – setting it on a path of lower growth and higher inflation – and that it would enable China to more successfully project its own values on to others.

Sources of conflict

A move towards greater isolationism by the US would impose significant costs on its own economy. But the costs of fracturing would be materially greater for *both* sides if the two blocs came into conflict. There are several potential triggers.

A key area of focus is the South China Sea. The infamous 'Nine-Dash Line' is a demarcation used by Beijing to assert its claims over a vast area of the Sea, including several disputed islands, reefs and waters. These claims overlap with those of several other countries in the region, including some, such as the Philippines and Vietnam, that fall under America's security umbrella. These territorial disputes therefore represent a key threat to regional and global stability.

In recent years, China has attempted to enforce its disputed claims by building artificial islands and military installations across the Sea. The US has responded by sending navy patrols through the same waters – prompting a predictably furious reaction in Beijing. Both sides are aware of the dangers of direct confrontation in the South China Sea and patrols are a way to assert interests without resorting to open conflict. But the risk of miscalculation remains high, especially in an environment of heightened tensions.

Another source of concern relates to the potential threats around cybersecurity and technological rivalry. Both the US and China are heavily involved in cyber operations, with allegations of hacking, intellectual property theft and cyber espionage on both sides. The competition in emerging technologies like AI, 5G and quantum computing adds another layer of tension. A significant cyberattack that is perceived as state-sponsored could lead to retaliatory actions. In a worst-case scenario, cyber operations could disrupt critical infrastructure, leading to military escalation.

Underpinning each of these potential areas of conflict is a single source of tension: China has not just emerged as an economic rival to the US, it has also emerged as a military rival. Beijing is now responsible for the world's second largest defence budget, its largest navy and some of its most advanced weaponry.

In most cases, the greatest danger lies in miscommunication or misinterpretation. The fact that both sides maintain a heavy military presence across the Asia-Pacific means there are countless ways in which an unintended military action or a misread diplomatic gesture could quickly spiral into conflict. However, there is one source of conflict where the risk lies less in miscommunication and more in overt action: Taiwan.

Taiwan – a short history

The history of Taiwan – known formerly as Formosa – is complex. Controlled by the Qing dynasty from the late seventeenth century, it was ceded to Japan in 1895 after the First Sino–Japanese War, before being placed under the administrative control of China in 1945 following Japan's defeat in the Second World War. Victory for Mao's Communists in the Chinese Civil War led to the establishment of the People's Republic of China (PRC) in 1949, after which the former Nationalist government of the Republic of China (RoC) retreated to Taiwan – taking with it a significant number of artistic and cultural treasures, along with the nation's gold reserves. This is the source of China's long-standing claim to sovereignty over Taiwan.

Taiwan's international position is ambiguous. The PRC asserts that there is only 'one China' and that Taiwan is an inseparable part of it. Taiwan itself has never officially declared independence. Most countries, including the United States, recognize the PRC as the sole legitimate government of China under the 'One China Policy'. However, many countries maintain unofficial relations with Taiwan and acknowledge its functioning as a de facto independent state.

This delicate diplomatic balance has led to three major crises in the Taiwan Strait since 1949. The first came in 1954 when the PRC began shelling the offshore islands of

Kinmen and Matsu, which are governed as part of Taiwan but are close to the Chinese mainland. In response, the US signed a mutual defence treaty with the Nationalist government in Taipei and the Seventh Fleet was deployed to help protect Taiwan. After months of escalation, tensions started to ease in 1955 following threats by some in the US government to use nuclear weapons against China. A second crisis then flared up in 1958 when the PRC renewed its artillery bombardment of the Kinmen and Matsu islands. Fierce battles with Taiwanese forces followed but once again the PRC stopped short of mounting a full-scale invasion. Finally, a visit to the US in 1995 by Taiwanese President Lee Teng-hui led the PRC to conduct a series of missile tests and exercises near Taiwan. In response, the US sent two aircraft battle groups to the area as a show of force.

Each of these crises was eventually de-escalated, but the tension over Taiwan's status has intensified following China's adoption of a more assertive foreign policy under President Xi. China's leadership has tied the reunification of Taiwan with the mainland to a goal of achieving 'national rejuvenation' by 2049 – the centennial of the Communist revolution. Crucially, China claims the right under its Anti-Secession Law to use 'non-peaceful means' if it no longer believes that 'peaceful reunification' is possible. Some US commanders believe an assault on Taiwan could now come as early as this decade. While it is unclear how America might respond to such action with Donald Trump in the White House, many view Taiwan as a tinderbox that will inevitably draw China and the US into direct conflict. If this were to happen then the economic costs would be the least of our concerns. But it is important to keep in mind that an assault on Taiwan could take a number of different forms and produce a number of different responses, each with different consequences.

An attack could take many forms

A Chinese attack on Taiwan conjures images of a D-Day-style amphibious assault on the island. In fact, not only does Taiwan's geography make this difficult – foggy waters and mountainous terrain do not lend themselves to such assaults – but there are many other ways that China might attempt to achieve its ultimate objective of coercing Taipei to submit to its political control.[6]

Taiwan controls more than 100 islands dotted across the Taiwan Strait and the South China Sea. Many have no permanent residents and lie hundreds of kilometres away from the main island – indeed, several of the largest lie much closer to mainland China. (See Figure 8.1.)

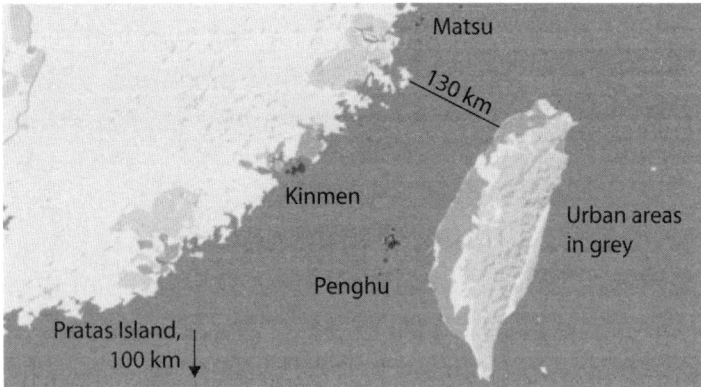

Figure 8.1 Taiwan and the Taiwan Strait

Source: Capital Economics, OpenStreetMap. This OpenStreetMap map is made available under the Open Database License: http://opendatacommons.org/licenses/odbl/1.0/. Any rights in individual contents of the database are licensed under the Database Contents License: http://opendatacommons.org/licenses/dbcl/1.0/

One way that China could put pressure on Taiwan would be for its military to seize a small, unpopulated, outlying island. This would allow Beijing to demonstrate its resolve while at the same time limiting the diplomatic blowback. The critical question would be whether Taiwan acquiesces or whether it fights back. China's military dominance means that a counter-offensive by Taiwan would be doomed, but since it would catalyse a response by Taiwan's allies then the risk of escalation would be high. Even if Taiwan did not fight back, China would surely find itself on the receiving end of US economic and financial sanctions.

Seizure of an island in the Taiwan Strait by China would be a more provocative act. There are three clusters of islands with sizeable populations in the Strait: Matsu and Kinmen (which were shelled in the 1954 Strait crisis) and Penghu, which is closer to the main island of Taiwan. Many analysts believe that a cross-Strait invasion would start with the seizure of these islands, along with others in the Strait with large Taiwanese military facilities, since it would protect invading forces from attack from the rear.

Accordingly, even if China did not intend to go further, the seizure of any one of these islands would feed suspicion that this was the first stage of an invasion plan. Taiwan would be compelled to respond and the US and other allies would be forced to make a decision about whether and how to provide support. Given the geopolitical stakes, global markets would take fright. Not only would there be a large pull-back in capital from Taiwan itself but there would be a flight out of 'risky' assets and into 'safe' assets such as the dollar, gold, the Swiss franc and US Treasuries. At the extreme, this could threaten financial stability in economies that depend on foreign capital to fund large external financing requirements, including the likes of Turkey, Egypt, South Africa and Romania. The effects would therefore be felt across the world.

Throttling Taiwan's economy

However, seizing territory is not the only way that China could assert greater control over Taiwan. An alternative would be to simply take control of its borders and, in the process, slowly throttle its economy. One way this could be done would be through a so-called 'quarantine operation'. This would entail China taking control of the customs territory of Taiwan and scrutinizing goods and people that came in and out of the country. This would not amount to a full blockade – most cross-border activity could continue. But China could decide which goods, people, ships and aircraft were allowed to cross the border and, where it deemed necessary, would be able to route them through the mainland. In doing so it would be able to deprive Taiwan of crucial military supplies coming into the country, and deprive the rest of the world of Taiwanese exports, the most critical of which are high-end semiconductors. This would not only force Taiwan to accept a significant loss of autonomy but, by choking off the supply of chips, China would also be able to inflict economic pain on its adversaries.

An alternative would be for China to enforce a full-scale blockade of Taiwan. This would be a more extreme step since it would cut off all air and sea routes in and out of the country. But it appears to have received serious consideration in Beijing. A recent report by the US Department of Defense on China's military capabilities stated that 'PLA writings describe a Joint Blockade Campaign in which the PRC would employ blockades of maritime and air traffic, including a cut-off of Taiwan's vital imports'.[7]

The objective would be to force Taiwan's capitulation. Its key vulnerability is a heavy reliance on imported food and, in particular, fuel. According to data published by the Taiwanese government, Taiwan produces about one-third of the calories that its people consume, with the remaining two-thirds coming from imports of food. But it is close to self-sufficient in many staples, including pork and rice, and the government maintains large stockpiles too. A survey conducted by the Council of Agriculture during the COVID-19 pandemic found that public and private rice stocks could meet Taiwan's needs for 18 months.

Taiwan's energy supply, however, would be much less resilient. Only 10–15 per cent of Taiwan's energy comes from domestically-produced fuels, renewable sources or nuclear power. Government and private stockpiles would provide a buffer for vehicle fuels. But Taiwan's electricity supply is heavily dependent on imported liquefied natural gas (LNG), which would be cut off in the event of a blockade. Stockpiles of LNG are much smaller than those for oil and food – importers are required to hold only eight days' supply in their 'security stockpile' – and would be vulnerable to Chinese attack. Taiwan's reliance on imported energy remains a key strategic weakness that would quickly be exposed in the event of a blockade.

Chip choke

For the rest of the world, the key vulnerability in the event of a blockade is its heavy reliance on semiconductors produced by Taiwan's chip giant, TSMC. Just over half of all the world's chips – and more than 90 per cent of its advanced chips – are produced in Taiwan.[8] These are the critical components that power the modern economy. Computers, phones, cars, household appliances, medical equipment, transport and telecommunications networks and most electrical devices simply would not work without them. The hit to the global economy if Taiwan's supply of chips was cut off would be catastrophic.

The COVID-19 pandemic provided a glimpse of the potential economic costs caused by disruptions to global chip supply. In the popular imagination this was caused by 'supply shortages'. The Biden administration even went as far as to commission a 250-page report on supply chain vulnerabilities that focussed on semiconductors. In fact, global chip supply was remarkably resilient throughout the pandemic. According to the Semiconductor Industry Association, capacity utilization at fabs increased throughout 2020 and chip sales rose by almost 7 per cent compared to 2019.[9] Instead, the problems were caused principally by pandemic-related shifts in demand. Lockdowns led to a surge in demand for chip-intensive products: firms and workers upgraded IT equipment to enable home-working, the shift online led to an increase in demand for servers from data centres, and, with the service sector largely shut down, households spent government stimulus checks on consumer electronics and gadgets.

This led to an associated surge in demand for chips, which was then compounded by errors in procurement. In the early days of the pandemic, anticipating a slump in sales, auto producers cut orders for chips. But when this failed to materialize and procurement teams resubmitted orders for chips they found that manufacturers had already reallocated production to other clients. The result was a chip choke that led to a collapse in auto production. It has been estimated that the industry produced 9.5 million fewer light vehicles globally in 2021 than would have been possible absent a shortage of chips.[10]

The economic costs of a blockade would be huge

Pandemic-related distortions to demand eventually eased, backlogs of orders for chips were fulfilled and auto production ultimately recovered. There was no permanent loss of output. But it would be a different story if there was a sustained reduction in (or disruption to) chip supply. Demand for goods and services fluctuates over the economic cycle but over the long term output is ultimately constrained by capacity on the supply side. If China were to restrict the supply of Taiwanese chips to the rest of the world, the economic costs would be enormous.

One estimate by economists at Bloomberg found that in the event of a year-long blockade of Taiwan by China, there would be a 5 per cent fall in global GDP. This would include a drop in Taiwan's GDP of 12 per cent and a hit to US GDP of 3.3 per cent.[11] Once again, these losses would be on a par with, and in some cases greater than, those caused by the 2008 Global Financial Crisis.

Of course, estimates of this kind are highly uncertain. For the US, the greatest cost might be its loss of strategic control over the production of high-end chips. The vast majority of the world's advanced chips are produced in Taiwan and a blockade would effectively leave them under China's control. The US and its allies would still dominate research and development, as well as the design of high-end chips. But it would be easier for China to catch up to the US in these areas with Taiwanese output under its control. A key technological strength of the US-bloc – its influence over the global development, design and production of semiconductors – would become a key strategic weakness.

Yet this would not be costless for China. It is also a large consumer of chips – indeed, it now spends more on imports of semiconductors each year than it does on imports of oil. A blockade of Taiwan would enable it to direct the flow of chips manufactured by TSMC to Chinese industry. But many of these chips go into products that are then re-exported to Western markets. In the event that it imposed a blockade on Taiwan, China would surely find itself subject to a broad range of economic and financial sanctions that, among other things, would lead to a much harder fracture with the US and which would cripple its exports. The potential sums involved are huge. The economists at Bloomberg found that a blockade of Taiwan would reduce China's GDP by just under 9 per cent in its first year – a hit equivalent to over $1.5trn.

All routes risk escalation

While there are various ways in which China could mount an assault against Taiwan, the key point is that they all come with a high risk of escalation. Ukraine's response to Russia's invasion illustrates that most governments will naturally fight back against any loss of sovereignty, even when attacked by a much larger neighbour. Indeed, from Taipei's perspective, fighting back may be seen as the only way to pull in support from its allies. This is as true in the scenario in which an outlying island is seized by China as it is in the event of a full-scale blockade. Accordingly, even if not the initial intention, each of these scenarios could easily escalate into a cross-Strait war. If this were the case, the risk of the US being drawn into conflict with China would be high.

Invasion would carry huge risks for China

The most provocative act would be for China to stage a full-scale invasion of Taiwan. Military experts differ on whether it has the capacity to do this successfully. In its latest assessment of China's military capabilities, the US Department of Defense concluded that 'a large-scale amphibious invasion would be one of the most complicated and difficult operations' for the PLA to carry out and that doing so would 'likely strain [China's] armed forces'.[12] This is principally because Taiwan's terrain favours defence. The east coast of the island consists of rocky cliffs, while the west coast is flanked by mud flats. There is only a handful of beaches that are suitable for bringing troops ashore and the time it would take China to amass the huge invasion force that would be required to mount an assault would provide Taiwan with a window to prepare its defences. Even if the troops landed successfully, they would still have to fight their way inland.

For this reason it is likely that an invasion of Taiwan would start with combined missile strikes and an airborne assault. The objective would be to catch Taiwan by surprise, knock out its key defences and critical infrastructure, and allow China to bring in troops, either by air or sea. But even this would be difficult to pull off. A surprise strike would have to be preceded by a major build-up of troops and equipment, which would be spotted by Taiwanese and US military reconnaissance. The sheer amount of resources that would be required means that any strike is likely to be telegraphed well in advance.

Set against this, China has a huge superiority in terms of the sheer volume of force it can bring to bear against Taiwan in the event of an invasion. It has about five times the number of fighter jets and warships, ten times the number of tanks and twelve times the number of troops. The question is how much of this resource Beijing is willing to spend in order to achieve its goal. During the Second World War the US developed a plan to mount an amphibious assault on Taiwan named Operation Causeway but quickly cancelled it after concluding that it would be too costly in terms of lives lost and resources required in order to defeat the far smaller Japanese force that at the time controlled the island. Given the central importance that Xi has attached to reunification with Taiwan as part of

China's 'national rejuvenation', the leadership in Beijing may reach a different conclusion today.

Costing catastrophe

A long-standing policy of 'strategic ambiguity' leaves open the question of how the US would respond in the event of a Chinese attack on Taiwan. This policy is designed to deter both China from attempting to invade Taiwan and Taiwan from declaring formal independence, which could provoke such an invasion. If the status quo was breached the US would be forced to reveal what this amounted to in practice. Washington would be faced with the biggest geo-political dilemma in generations: engage in direct military action to defend Taiwan and be pulled into a conflict with China, or provide support from the sidelines and risk China becoming the dominant power in the Asia-Pacific region. The re-election of Donald Trump on a promise to challenge China's rise but also keep the US out of global wars adds an additional element of uncertainty around the US response should China attack Taiwan during his term in office.

Even if America opted to provide support from the sidelines, it is hard to imagine that there wouldn't be a serious rupture in economic relations between the US-bloc and China. The package of measures enacted by the US and its allies against Russia following its invasion of Ukraine offers some insight into what this would be likely to comprise. Sanctions would be wide-ranging. It is likely that many of China's assets in Western banks would be frozen and that its access to the US dollar – and thereby the global financial system – would be limited.

Western firms operating in China would face retaliatory actions, including asset freezes, by Beijing.

The outbreak of war would inevitably hit the production of semiconductors in Taiwan, creating a supply shock for both sides. Trade between the blocs would also be restricted. The economic damage from a hard decoupling would be greater for China – its economy is more export-oriented and nearly two-thirds of its exports go to the US-bloc. But the shock for the US and its allies would also be substantial. China is an order of magnitude more important than Russia to the global trading system.

The Bloomberg analysis suggests that a war over Taiwan would create a $10trn hit to the global economy. This would comprise a 40 per cent fall in Taiwan's GDP, a near-17 per cent fall in China's GDP and a 6.7 per cent fall in US GDP. The authors estimate that Global GDP would fall by 10 per cent.

In truth, estimating the hit to GDP misses the point: the world's two major powers, each with large nuclear arsenals, would be at high risk of war. If they came into direct conflict, a breakdown in economic and financial relations between the US and China would not be the main concern. But it would lead to a hard and lasting decoupling between both sides. Most trade would stop and most assets on both sides would be seized, creating financial chaos. The rupture in the global economy would be long-lasting. It is possible that it could take generations to re-establish relations.

Worst outcome is made in Taiwan

The upshot is that there is no scenario in which a Chinese assault on Taiwan would produce good outcomes for both sides – and there are several where it would produce extremely bad ones. From an economic perspective, the consequences will be determined by three things. The first is whether any action by China against Taiwan can be contained and prevented from spiralling into something more serious. This would be hard and the response of the US would be critical.

The second is the effect that any action has on shipments of Taiwanese semiconductors. Absent a direct conflict, this is the key channel of economic contagion to the rest of the world. In the long term, a major strategic risk for the US is that China gains greater control over Taiwanese chip production and thus undermines a key prop to US technological supremacy.

Finally, regardless of the exact form it took, any action by Beijing against Taiwan would almost certainly lead to a more significant fracture between the US and China. Even the ideal outcome from Beijing's perspective of Taiwan capitulating quickly would require the US to accept that China had become the dominant power in the Asia-Pacific region. And even if it was prepared to accept a diminished position in the world, it is still likely that the US would attempt to shore up its own anti-China alliance and impose harder barriers on inter-bloc flows of trade, finance and technology. There are several paths that would lead to a more significant fracture between the US and China, each with substantially higher economic costs for both sides. But the most serious of all of them would start with disruption to the status quo over Taiwan.

CHAPTER 9

What Lies Ahead

This is a book about the end of globalization and what comes next. It is a story about the rise of China to become a peer challenger to the US and the consequences that this will have for the way that the global economy is organized. The three decades that followed the end of the Cold War were a period of integration and cooperation. I have argued that the coming decades will be marked by a deepening superpower rivalry and the fracturing of US–China relations. The way in which this fracturing evolves will shape the world in which we live. But what will that world look like in 2040 and how should we prepare? Let us start with the big picture.

The big picture

The critical factors that will determine the economic consequences of fracturing over the next decade will be the speed at which the US and China pull apart, how broad and hard the split becomes, and the extent to which other countries are dragged in. As things stand, despite increasingly heated rhetoric, a reasonable base case is that fracturing proceeds in a managed way and is contained to strategically important sectors. If this is the case then many of the subsequent changes to the ways in which businesses operate and we live our everyday lives will be subtle rather than pronounced. Forecasts of an impending collapse in world trade will be proved wrong. Goods, services and capital will continue to move across borders.

Instead a contained form of fracturing will leave its mark in other important ways. Since the process is being driven by governments, it is the change in the prevailing attitudes of policymakers that will be critical in shaping the type of fracturing we get. At root, the world will be one in which governments will attach greater priority to economic and national security when setting policy.

One way that this will manifest itself is in greater pressure on governments to spend more on defence. This will add to existing long-term pressures on the public finances from ageing societies in Western economies. The members of NATO have pledged to increase spending on defence to 2 per cent of GDP. If they were to pledge to increase this to 3 per cent of GDP – which is just below what the US currently spends – then it would cost the UK an additional $35bn, France an additional $31bn and Germany an additional $45bn. If defence spending was to increase to 4 per cent of GDP – which was commonplace before the end of the Cold War – then it would cost the US an additional $285bn, the UK an additional $70bn, France an additional $62bn and Germany an additional $90bn. The tax burden is already at a post-war high in several countries, including the UK. But with the demands on government likely to grow, a fractured world is likely to be one in which the tax burden increases further.

However, while fracturing is being driven by governments, most of the consequences will be transmitted through the private sector. Most obviously, fracturing will affect the way that firms organize their supply chains. Maximizing efficiencies will no longer be the only game in town. Corporate leaders will instead attach greater importance to resilience. In boardrooms across the world, executives will pay more attention to potential choke points in their supply chains. It will become more common for firms to secure inputs from multiple sources despite the higher cost of doing so.

Over and above this, a combination of legislation and government pressure will mean that national security considerations are likely to play a much greater role in corporate decisions over the location of production and the sourcing of components. In some cases, this will mean that multinationals serving the US market will move production out of China. As I set out in Chapter 4, this is most likely to happen in areas where it is perceived that ties with China could compromise national security or technological leadership. These include:

- semiconductors;

- telecommunications and the associated infrastructure;

- quantum computing;

- AI products and related infrastructure, including data centres;

- key areas of green technology, including electric vehicles in the US;

- critical minerals;

- pharmaceuticals and medical goods; and

- various 'smart goods' that connect us to the internet, including smart phones, tablets and watches.

These shifts will form part of a broader bifurcation in global technology flows. Technological leadership underpins global economic leadership and so, as fracturing deepens, the US and China will each take steps to prevent the other from stealing a march in key technologies. The past 30 years has been a period in which new technologies have dispersed quickly across borders. Wind the clock forward two decades however and it is likely that the cars we drive and phones and software we use will be determined by the bloc in which we live.

Meanwhile, at a global level, fracturing will represent a final nail in the coffin for multilateralism. To the extent that international deals are struck these will be on narrow issues and agreed within blocs rather than across all countries. Major institutions such as the World Trade Organization and the IMF will continue to lose influence. In a fractured world, challenges that require collective action – most notably meeting targets to cut emissions and tackle climate change – will become much harder to tackle.

So much for the big picture. How will fracturing affect the economic prospects for individual countries? What follows is a short guide as to how the world's major economies and key regions and groups of economies are likely to fare over the next decade. The objective is not to provide a detailed economic forecast but rather to draw together the key arguments I have made in this book to provide a thumbnail sketch of what the economic landscape for each might look like in 2040. In doing so, I assume once again that fracturing is contained to areas deemed to be of strategic importance.

United States: starting from a position of strength

America has three core strengths in a fractured world: the size and economic diversity of its own economy and also of its allies; its technological leadership in a broad range of areas, particularly research and development; and the central role the dollar plays within the global financial system. These strengths – particularly its relations with allies – will be severely tested under a second Trump administration. The most important question hanging over the long-run outlook for the US is whether it squanders its strong starting position.

Despite President Trump's fiery rhetoric, it is likely that America will continue to conduct a significant amount of trade with China in basic goods, and that it will continue to run a bilateral trade deficit. But by 2040 it is likely that the US will have taken substantial steps to cut out Chinese technology from critical supply chains. It will have barred the use of all but the most basic products that use Chinese-produced semiconductors; restrictions will have been tightened on the use of Chinese components that comprise the 'Internet of Things'; Chinese electric vehicles will not be seen on US streets. Some of these goods and the component parts that go into them will be produced in the US.

The current push to produce high-end semiconductors in America will bear fruit. But in most cases where supply is moved out of China, it is likely to shift instead to friendly countries. Trade with other major emerging markets will also come under strain during the current Trump administration but over the long run a major pullback in trade between the US and the likes of Mexico, Vietnam and India is unlikely and it is a reasonable bet that trade ties in some geopolitically sensitive areas will deepen.

The populist push to 'reshore' manufacturing jobs is therefore likely to fail. By 2040, the share of total employment accounted for by manufacturing is likely to be either unchanged or slightly lower than it is today. But this will not be an impediment to economic prosperity. America's strong position in technology and innovation means that it will remain at the forefront of new technological breakthroughs. Of the world's major economies, it is likely that the US will reap the most benefits from the AI revolution. GDP is likely to grow by something like 2.5–3.0 per cent a year over the next decade – a fraction higher than the average recorded over the past decade.

Forecasts of the impending demise of the dollar will continue to surface in investment research and op-eds over the coming decade. But the dollar will remain the world's most important currency and the US will continue to provide the financial plumbing for the global economy. This will give it significant leverage over its adversaries. The use of financial sanctions will become more common.

America will face two principal challenges over the next decade or so in the context of fracturing. The first will be to overcome China's dominance over the supply of critical minerals needed in the modern economy. Efforts will be made to build alliances with key producers in Africa and Latin America, but progress will be slow and supply interruptions will be common. As a result, while fracturing itself is unlikely to cause a surge in US inflation over the coming decade, more frequent disruptions to the supply side of America's economy may mean that it becomes more volatile.

The greatest challenge, however, will be to resist the temptation to turn inwards and embrace isolationism. If the US can keep its allies onside over the coming decades, it is highly likely that it will remain the world's largest economy in 2040. In contrast, an isolationist shift would alienate America's allies – which are one of its key sources of strength in a fractured world – and set it on a path of lower growth and higher inflation.

China: fracturing will compound structural headwinds

America's strengths in a fractured world are mirrored by China's weaknesses. China's allies are smaller and less economically diverse than America's; China remains critically dependent on the US-bloc for key foundational technologies (notably high-end chips); and China's large external surplus means that it will have little option but to hold large amounts of dollar-denominated assets.

The economic backdrop against which fracturing is taking place is also very different in China compared to the US. While America has experienced a decade or more of tepid growth following the Global Financial Crisis, it may now experience a period of faster growth driven by AI. In contrast, having experienced several decades of rapid growth that has raised expectations of sustained increases in prosperity, China's economy is now facing structural headwinds.

Fast forward to 2040 and it is likely that China will remain an export powerhouse. It will still be the world's largest producer of most consumer goods and the hub around which most global manufacturing is oriented. At the same time, it will remain a global leader in many areas of technology. It is hard to say what this will include without just extrapolating from today, but it is a very good bet that China will continue to lead in key areas of green technology including batteries.

However, as I noted earlier, Chinese exporters will also find that they have been cut off from US markets in areas that are deemed to be strategically important or sensitive. At the same time, it is likely that China will have also been blocked from accessing a wider range of advanced technology produced by the US and its allies. The most important of these is advanced semiconductors but this could also extend to areas such as software.

China will take steps to develop these technologies domestically and, while progress will be slower than might otherwise have been the case, in most cases it will be successful. However, doing so will require China's leadership to double down on a state-led, investment-intensive model of growth that is already hitting the buffers. The next decade is therefore likely to be one of declining productivity growth and thus slower income growth. Coupled with a deepening demographic squeeze this could pull down GDP growth to just 2 per cent a year.

The result is that by 2040 China will be something of a Jekyll and Hyde economy. Pockets of global leadership in some areas of manufacturing technology will coexist with much of the population living at much lower incomes than in the West. The economy will grow at a substantially slower rate than in the past decade. Managing the social and political strains that this creates will become a growing priority for the leadership in Beijing.

Europe: managed decoupling

Social, political and security ties mean that in a fractured world Europe will clearly align with the US. However, several countries, notably Germany, have a strong commercial relationship with China that they will naturally seek to protect. And the fact that economic growth across Europe will remain low relative to the US will add to caution about taking radical measures to disrupt the status quo.

This being the case, it is likely that Europe will adopt an approach of 'managed decoupling' with respect to China – restricting ties in some areas, but allowing business to continue as usual in others. Where the balance ends up landing over the next decade will be contingent on events and, in particular, the actions of China and the US.

Outright aggression by Beijing, or even attempts to influence European society and politics, would elicit a strong push-back from Brussels and result in a harder break. But the US will also play a key role in determining where Europe draws the line. For example, if Washington was to mandate that Europe cut out certain Chinese components from its national infrastructure, or that it restricts the export of certain goods to China, in order that it remains under America's security umbrella or is shielded from punitive tariffs, then European governments would reluctantly comply.

What this means in practice is that by 2040 it is likely that Europe will have broken from China in some areas but will have maintained ties in others. The break is most likely to happen in high-tech areas, including semiconductor technology, computing, pharmaceuticals and advanced manufacturing. But the bar to cutting out Chinese-produced batteries and electric vehicles will be higher in Europe than in the US. And trade in many areas such as machinery and other capital goods may be broadly unchanged from today. Chinese investment will be tolerated rather than encouraged, but policymakers in Brussels and national capitals will take a more pragmatic and less ideological approach than their counterparts in the US. It is likely that Europe will rely heavily on Chinese technology and investment to achieve its climate goals.

This will strain relations with Washington but won't push Europe out of America's bloc. Likewise, while Beijing will continue to court strong-man leaders in Europe, such as Viktor Orbán in Hungary, this is unlikely to fundamentally alter the region's geopolitical orientation.

The fundamental point in all of this is that, despite talk of 'strategic autonomy' in areas of foreign relations, Europe is unlikely to push a strong agenda when it comes to fracturing. The focus will remain on managing the region's many domestic challenges: ageing populations, high public debt burdens, weak productivity growth and incomplete monetary union. The scale of the task was laid bare in a 2024 report by Mario Draghi, the former Prime Minister of Italy and head of the European Central Bank (ECB), in which he estimated that Europe needed to raise investment by €800bn a year in order to keep pace with the US and China.[1] In practice, Europe is likely to fall well short of this figure, not least because it will be slow to move towards creating a fiscal union which would give it the powers to raise funds on that scale.

Come 2040 it is likely that Europe will be a region of high living standards but low economic growth; a region of highly open economies that have cut ties with China in some areas but continue to trade heavily with it in others; and a region that is still firmly allied to the US.

India: an era of optimism

Fracturing will test India's long-standing tradition of non-alignment – that is to say, the policy of not taking sides in geopolitical conflicts. As a major emerging economy and significant power in Asia, India will seek common ground with Beijing on some issues. However, a long-running border dispute will remain a strain on relations with China, and New Delhi will become increasingly aware of the potential advantages of positioning itself as a reliable partner to the US in a fractured world. While India will try to straddle both blocs, if pushed it will probably lean towards the US. Over the next decade it will become one of the world's most exciting growth stories.

India has several strengths. Unlike China, its demographic outlook is good. Whereas China's working-age population is forecast to grow by 2 per cent by 2040, India's is forecast to grow by over 15 per cent.[2] India is also relatively poor – GDP per capita is about 40 per cent of what it is in China.[3] This may sound like a peculiar source of strength but, to flip this on its head, a low starting point means that India has plenty of scope to undergo a period of rapid 'catch-up growth' as incomes converge to those of richer economies.

There remain several barriers to development. India's infrastructure is poor by emerging market standards. Its road, rail, port and logistics infrastructure is antiquated, leading to high transportation costs and frequent delays; its housing stock remains inadequate; its power supply intermittent. India's byzantine public sector creates unnecessary impediments to growth: private investment, for example, is held back by a thicket of red tape. Barriers to trade and foreign investment also remain high by the standards of other emerging markets in Asia.

Crucially, however, India's government appears to understand the problem. Progress has been slow, but it has embarked on reforms to liberalize labour markets, dismantle price controls, reform and modernize public services and open up to foreign investment. This is helping to foster the image of a government that has increasingly authoritarian inclinations, but is nonetheless market-friendly. Critically, it remains friendly towards the US – and will therefore be one of several obvious destinations for firms to relocate plants to in instances where fracturing leads to production being shifted out of China.

Over the past two decades India's growth has been propelled by its service sector, particularly in business support and computing. This will remain a critical sector. But over the next decade it is likely to be complemented by the gradual development of the manufacturing sector. India will not rival China's broad manufacturing capabilities. But it will develop pockets of strength in areas such as the production of telecoms equipment and consumer electronics. The result will be that its economy will continue to grow at rates of 6 per cent or so a year – lifting it towards middle-income status and making it by some distance the world's best performing major economy.

Commodity producers: in a tug of war

There is a theory about natural resource demand over the next decade that goes something like this: as the green transition accelerates, demand for oil and gas will inevitably fall whereas demand for metals and minerals used in green technologies, such as nickel, zinc, copper and lithium, will inevitably increase. According to this view, fossil fuels are yesterday's news – the commodities of the future will be the various metals and minerals that are inputs to everything from batteries to wind turbines that will be the critical commodities of the future. As a result, the major oil-producing countries, notably Saudi Arabia and other Gulf nations, will diminish in importance and economic prowess, while the major mineral producers – Chile, Brazil, South Africa and many others in Latin America and sub-Saharan Africa – will be the commodity powerhouses of the future.

This has a grain of truth but it is overly simplistic. The reality is that all commodities, with perhaps the exception of the dirtiest fossil fuels such as coal, will be in high demand over the coming decade. This being the case, commodity producers will find themselves at the centre of a tussle between Washington and Beijing to secure supplies of natural resources over the next decade. This will be an important sub-plot to US–China fracturing.

The question of when global demand for fossil fuels will peak is a matter of intense debate. OPEC (which has skin in the game) does not expect oil demand to peak at all in its long-term forecasts; the International Energy Agency believes it will come as soon as 2029.[4] Even so, the IEA believes that by the start of the next decade global oil demand will still be higher than it is today. Meanwhile, natural gas consumption is forecast to climb further. Despite efforts to "green" economies, the world will continue to consume large amounts of fossil fuels.

The world's largest oil producers can be split into three camps: those that sit in the China-bloc (Russia, Iran, Venezuela), those that sit in the US-bloc (Colombia, Mexico but most importantly the US itself) and those that are attempting to straddle both blocs (notably Saudi Arabia and the United Arab Emirates). The map of global oil production is therefore already spread fairly evenly across blocs. Despite this, China is likely to intensify efforts to strengthen ties with Saudi Arabia, the major power in the Gulf and most influential member of the OPEC cartel. This will be only partially successful – strong security ties to America will continue to exert a powerful pull back to the US-bloc.

If global oil demand peaks around the end of this decade and then starts to fall, then it follows that the export income earned by the world's major oil producers must fall too. This will either happen through lower prices or lower volumes. Either way, this will translate into slower income growth in their economies. By 2040, GDP growth in the Gulf nations could slow to 2.0–2.5 per cent a year, down from rates of around 4 per cent seen over the past decade. At the same time, the large current account surpluses run by the major oil producers in the Gulf will shrink. These countries will continue to hold large amounts of overseas assets – and since these will be largely invested in Western markets, they will act as another pull towards the US-bloc. But the speed at which Saudi Arabia and others in the region accumulate foreign assets will have slowed significantly by 2040.

While the global energy map is spread relatively evenly across blocs, China's investment-intensive growth model means that it has much stronger economic ties to the major metals and minerals producers than the US. But that does not mean that these countries will necessarily become strong allies of China. Political systems in most of these countries are very different from China. The most important are all democracies. As a result, they won't see eye to eye over issues around human rights. What's more, their citizens tend to look towards the West rather than Beijing. Most countries in Latin America and Sub-Saharan Africa have stronger social and cultural ties to the US and Europe than they do to China.

All of this, coupled with the fact that the minerals they produce will become increasingly important within the global economy, means that over the next decade these countries are likely to find themselves at the centre of a tug of war between China and the US. In some cases, this will be encouraged by political leaders. After all, while existing ties to China are strong, there is a strategic reason for producers not to allow Beijing exclusive access to their commodity deposits: doing so would only incentivize the US to build extraction elsewhere, resulting in an eventual loss of global market share.

As demand for minerals needed to sustain the green transition increases, the countries that produce them will see significant amounts of investment and, as production comes online, substantial export growth. This in turn will mean that they are likely to record higher rates of economic growth than the major oil producers in the Gulf. At the same time, however, this will entrench commodity-led growth models that are vulnerable to rent seeking and governance problems, and from which it is notoriously difficult to sustain rapid productivity growth over long periods. To the extent that these economies manage to diversify away from the mining of metals and minerals, it is likely to be towards associated activities such as refining. Some economies in Africa will manage growth of 4–5 per cent a year over the next decade, in part due to rapid population growth. But most commodity producers in Latin America will grow at slower rates of 2–3 per cent or so. While commodity producers will find themselves courted by both Beijing and Washington, this will not diminish the challenges that have dogged economic development in these countries over the past 50 years.

Manufacturing emerging markets: positive stories but no new China

The next decade will be one of opportunity for emerging market manufacturing economies. Part of this opportunity will stem from the US taking steps to relocate production from China in geopolitically sensitive areas – although this may not materialize to a significant extent under the current Trump presidency. But it will also result from Western firms seeking to 'de-risk' their supply chains more generally and diversify the location of inputs along them. By 2040, it is likely that companies based in the West will have expanded capacity in friendly countries at the expense of expanding operations in China.

But investment in manufacturing sectors will not only come from the West. Chinese firms themselves may also seek to expand production in these countries both to serve Western markets or to circumvent protectionist measures enacted by the US and others. For example, the Chinese car maker BYD is setting up production facilities in Hungary and Turkey in order to serve the European market.

The key beneficiaries are likely to be those economies that can position themselves as reliable allies of the US, have an existing manufacturing base and are located close to key markets, particularly the US and Europe. The winners over the next decade are likely to be Vietnam, Mexico, Turkey and manufacturers in central east Europe, including Poland, Czechia and Hungary. All are likely to see high levels of investment in manufacturing.

This will spur debate as to which economy will be the 'next China'. There won't be one. China is unique in terms of the size of its population, its industrial base and the resources it can put to work in manufacturing. Instead, countries are likely to develop specialisms that build on areas of existing strengths. Mexico and the economies of Central and Eastern Europe already have large automotive sectors and so are likely to develop as regional hubs for electric vehicles and battery production. Vietnam has existing strengths in electronics and is likely to become an increasingly important centre for the production of high-tech consumer goods and telecommunications equipment. None of these economies will challenge China in terms of the scope and reach of the manufacturing base. But over the next decade, they will be among the few success stories that result from global fracturing.

Growth rates among emerging market manufacturers are likely to vary. Some lower-income countries like Vietnam could sustain growth rates of 5–6 per cent a year for some time; higher-income emerging markets with poorer demographic outlooks – like those in Central and Eastern Europe – are likely to expand at a more modest 2–3 per cent a year. But one thing these countries will have in common will be that they will continue to see their income levels converge towards those of developed economies. After all, moving up the manufacturing value-added chain has been the one sure-fire way to raise productivity levels and sustainably climb the development ladder. This process is likely to reinforce ties with Western-leaning economies.

The world in 2040

The various ways in which fracturing will shape developments in different countries and regions over the next decade will have significant consequences for the global economic hierarchy. Most analysts argue that it is a matter of when not if China overtakes the US to become the world's largest economy measured at market exchange rates. Indeed, it is the seemingly unstoppable rise of China's economy that is driving fracturing in the first place. But projections that China will inevitably overtake the US fall into the trap of what I call 'straight-line forecasting'. They extrapolate the past into the future and in doing so assume that tomorrow will look a lot like today. As this book makes clear, it won't.

China's population is admittedly vast. At 1.4 billion it is more than four times that of America's. This means that China's overall GDP would surpass that of America if its GDP per person rises to just one-quarter of that of the US. In other words, the sheer size of China's population means that it could remain a relatively poor country and still become the world's largest economy.

The problem, as I have set out, is that income growth in China is set to slow as the consequences of fracturing compound the existing constraints within its economic model. If China's GDP growth rate slows to 2 per cent by the end of this decade and the US continues to grow at around 2.0–2.5 per cent, both of which are plausible, then China will never overtake the US to become the world's largest economy. Instead, China will close the gap on the US over the next few years before starting to fall away by the end of this decade – leaving America as the world's largest economy and, by virtue of the dollar's dominance, the steward of its financial system.

Moving up the rankings

The likelihood that the US will maintain its place as the world's largest economy is an example of something that *won't* change as a result of fracturing. Likewise, in the world I have described, Germany, France and the UK are likely to remain comfortably within the ten large economies over the next decade. The same is true of Japan.

The big change is likely to be India. If it can capitalize on the opportunities provided by fracturing and sustain annual growth rates of 6 per cent or so by the end of the decade it will, by some distance, be the world's third largest economy when measured at market exchange rates. By 2040, it is likely to account for just over 5 per cent of global GDP. To be clear, this would still make its economy considerably smaller than China's (which by this time may account for close to 15 per cent of global GDP). It will therefore lack the heft to challenge the US and China as a third global economic superpower. But the size and rapid growth of India's economy will encourage New Delhi to play a more independent role in the world. Washington and Beijing will make increasing efforts to court its support on key issues.

Fracturing will also allow Vietnam to climb the global economic rankings over the coming decade. By 2040 it is likely to have established itself as one of the world's 25 largest economies. Other large emerging economies that could benefit from fracturing such as Mexico and Poland are richer and so have a lower trend rate of growth, meaning they are less likely to surge up the global economic rankings. However, in ten years' time Poland will have converged further with richer economies in Western Europe and Mexico is likely to have achieved high-income status (defined by the World Bank in 2023 as a GDP per capita above $14,005).

At the other end of the scale, because fracturing is likely to entrench commodity-based growth models across Africa and much of Latin America, economic progress in these regions will be slower. Africa will continue to experience rapid population growth but income growth will be much slower. Brazil and South Africa will remain important regional powers, but neither will become a top five global economic power. Meanwhile Russia will continue to slide down the list of the world's largest economies. By 2040, it is possible that it will have dropped out of the top 20.

A shift in the narrative

These shifts become more stark when viewed through the lens of blocs. The economies that align with China have over the past 30 years accounted for an ever greater share of global GDP. In 1990, China and its current close allies made up 6 per cent of global GDP; today they account for over 25 per cent. The counterpart to this is that the share of global GDP accounted for by the US and its close allies has fallen from 85 per cent to 65 per cent. Over the next decade, the share of global GDP accounted for by the China-bloc is likely to stabilize and possibly edge lower. Conversely, the share accounted for by the US-bloc is likely to flatten out at its current level.

This will transform the narrative around fracturing. For the past 20 years or so there has been a perception that the US and its allies are in inexorable decline, in large part because their share of global output was falling. In contrast, China and its allies have been resurgent. If the share of global GDP accounted for by both the US and its allies and China and its allies stabilizes then it will become much harder to make the case that the West is in relative decline.

The path ahead

Of course, all of this is based on the significant assumption that fracturing will be both a slow and contained process. As I have set out, there are several ways in which it could evolve that would have more serious economic consequences. If the US retreated into isolationism, the relative decline of the West would accelerate. By 2040 it is likely that China would be the world's largest economy and the US would have experienced a decade of sclerotic growth and high inflation.

Meanwhile, if the US and China were drawn into conflict, the economic consequences would be devastating for both sides. Quantifying this is extremely difficult but it is reasonable to assume that the economic shock would be at least as great as that of the 2008 Global Financial Crisis.

Some argue that faced with these costs and risks, policymakers in Washington and Beijing must rebuild bilateral relations and our collective faith in multilateralism. As I hope I have made clear in this book, this would benefit everyone, not just citizens of the US and China. A great power rivalry benefits nobody and comes with significant economic, social and political costs for most. It also creates the very real risk that the two superpowers are pulled into a disastrous conflict with devastating human costs.

However, calls for a return to the previous era of multilateral cooperation overlook the fact that there are significant factions in both the US and China that are actively pushing for a split. Attempting to re-establish old norms ignores the fundamental frictions that have built on both sides. Instead, fracturing is better viewed as a process that must be managed. The responsibility for doing so will fall to all of us.

Firms across the globe must assess their vulnerability to splits in the areas I have laid out in this book. They must adapt, diversifying supply chains, forging new partnerships, and shifting production where necessary in order to reduce exposure to geopolitical tensions. Flexibility and foresight will be essential. Those companies that act pre-emptively to build resilience will thrive, while those that cling to outdated models risk decline in this increasingly uncertain environment.

For investors, fracturing will demand a shift in strategy. Countries – and sectors within countries – that once promised strong returns now carry significant risks. Western investments in Chinese technology serve as a clear warning: what once seemed like sound strategy can quickly become perilous as geopolitical tensions rise. Inter-bloc investment in private markets, where rules are more opaque, may be particularly hazardous. Yet, as I have set out, fracturing will also create new opportunities in economies that stand to benefit from these shifts. Investors must realign their portfolios, moving away from areas vulnerable to fracture and towards regions and industries that are better positioned to weather, and even thrive in, a world of greater geo-economic competition. The ability to identify risks and pivot quickly will be crucial. But equally, investors must not fall foul of seemingly simple and straightforward theories about the financial consequences of fracturing – most obviously that China's rise will inevitably challenge the dollar's role at the heart of the global economy.

Central banks, too, will face new challenges. Global supply chains, once prized for their efficiency, may now falter under geopolitical pressure, leading to sudden price shocks. Policymakers must be prepared. Inflation shocks caused by fracturing will arise from dislocation caused to the supply side of economies. Diagnosing whether this dislocation is temporary or permanent will be critical. If it is temporary then tightening policy in response would be both unnecessary and damaging. In this book I have argued that a fractured world is likely to be one in which inflation is more volatile but not necessarily higher. Faced with this, the core objective of central banks must be to anchor inflation expectations. In order to achieve this they must double down on inflation targets and resist calls to expand their remits to include other objectives such as greening economies.

Yet, the greatest burden falls on governments. In this fractured age, the risks are not just economic but existential. As global competition intensifies and the pillars of the globalization era erode, the danger of escalation looms large. It may not be possible to reconcile differences between the US and China, but it is possible to contain them. The goal must be to prevent divisions from spiralling into open conflict. In order to do so, channels of communication between Washington and Beijing – and between blocs more generally – must be kept open. Governments on both sides of the divide must understand the drivers of fracturing and recognize the risks, ensuring that competition does not descend into disaster.

The era of hyper-globalization has ended, and US–China fracturing is now a reality. The critical task is to manage this shift carefully. Resisting it is futile; instead, we must focus on avoiding the worst outcomes by understanding the forces driving global division. I hope this book offers a roadmap for navigating this fractured world.

Notes

Prologue

1 Ren, Z. (2001) 'My father and mother'. Available at: https://xinsheng.huawei.com/next/#/detail?uuid=916313593418559503.
2 World Bank, 'Tariff rate, applied, weighted mean, all products (%)'. Available at: https://data.worldbank.org/indicator/TM.TAX.MRCH.WM.AR.ZS.
3 Gartner (2019) 'Gartner says global smartphone sales stalled in the fourth quarter of 2018', 21 February. Available at: https://www.gartner.com/en/newsroom/press-releases/2019-02-21-gartner-says-global-smartphone-sales-stalled-in-the-fourth-quart#:~:text=Global%20sales%20of%20smartphones%20to,the%20first%20quarter%20of%202016.
4 Yang, Y. (2019) 'Huawei shrugs off US sanctions as sales grow 18%', *Financial Times*, 31 December.
5 Zoellick, R. (2005) 'Whither China: From membership to responsibility', Speech to National Committee on US–China Relations, New York City, 21 September.
6 Warburton, M. (2021) 'Key events in Huawei CFO Meng Wanzhou's extradition case', Reuters, 24 September.
7 Counterpoint Research (2024) 'China smartphone sales remain in Black on Huawei, HONOR, Xiaomi Outperformance', 23 April.
8 Huawei Investment & Holding Company (2023) 2023 Annual Report.

9 United Nations Trade and Development (UNCTAD) (2024) 'Global trade update (March 2024)'. Available at: https://unctad.org/publication/global-trade-update-march-2024.

Chapter 1

1 International Monetary Fund (2024) Direction of Trade Statistics. Author's calculations. Available at: https://data.imf.org.

2 Marley, P. and Stein, J. (2017) 'Foxconn announces $10 billion investment in Wisconsin and up to 13,000 jobs', *Milwaukee Journal Sentinel*, 26 July. Available at: https://eu.jsonline.com/story/news/2017/07/26/scott-walker-heads-d-c-trump-prepares-wisconsin-foxconn-announcement/512077001/.

3 Martinez, S. (2023) 'A short timeline of Foxconn's plans and development in Wisconsin', *Milwaukee Journal Sentinel*, 11 November. Available at: https://eu.jsonline.com/story/money/business/2023/11/10/what-happened-to-foxconn-in-wisconsin-a-timeline/71535498007/.

4 Ahlbers, T. and Uebele, M. (2015) 'The global impact of the Great Depression', London School of Economics Working Paper 218/2015.

5 Fukuyama, F. (2012). *The end of history and the last man*. Penguin.

6 International Monetary Fund (2024) World Economic Outlook Database, gross domestic product, current prices, US dollars and gross domestic product per capita, constant prices, national currency. Author's calculations. Available at: https://www.imf.org/en/Publications/SPROLLs/world-economic-outlook-databases.

7 International Monetary Fund (2024) World Economic Outlook Database, gross domestic product, current prices, US dollars. Author's calculations. Available at: https://www.imf.org/en/Publications/SPROLLs/world-economic-outlook-databases.

8 International Monetary Fund (2024) Direction of Trade Statistics. Author's calculations. Available at: https://data.imf.org.

9 Roy, R. and Yang, J. (2023) 'Apple aims to make a quarter of the world's iPhones in India', *The Wall Street Journal*, 8 December.

10 Capital Economics (2019) 'Lessons from the history of globalization', October, p 2.

11 US Treasury (2024) 'Major foreign holders of Treasury securities', Treasury International Capital System Data. Available at: https://ticdata.treasury.gov/resource-center/data-chart-center/tic/Documents/slt_table5.html.

12 Bank for International Settlements (2022) 'Survey of foreign exchange and over-the-counter (OTC) derivatives markets in 2022', Triennial Central Bank, 27 October, p 3.

13 Author's calculations using IMF Coordinated Portfolio Investment Survey, IMF Coordinated Direct Investment Survey and BIS Locational Banking Statistics. Available at: https://data.bis.org/topics/LBS and https://data.imf.org.

14 Capital Economics (2022) *The Fracturing of the Global Economy*, 12 October, p 28.

15 Eurostat (2024) 'Imports of oil and petroleum products by partner country – monthly data', 'Imports of natural gas by partner country – monthly data', Eurostat database. Available at: https://ec.europa.eu/eurostat.

16 Critical Minerals Alliance (2024). Available at: https://www.crmalliance.eu/gallium and https://www.crmalliance.eu/germanium.

17 Australian Strategic Policy Institute (2023) 'ASPI's Critical Technology Tracker, top 5 country visual snapshot', 22 September.

18 United States Department of Commerce (2024) 'Citing national security concerns Biden–Harris administration announces inquiry into connected vehicles', 29 February.

19 Semiconductor Industry Association, *2024 SIA Factbook*, p 3.

20 United Nations (2023) 'India to overtake China as world's most populous country in April 2023, United Nations projects', 23 April.

21 International Monetary Fund (2024) World Economic Outlook Database, gross domestic product, current prices, US dollars. Author's calculations and forecasts. Available at: https://www.imf.org/en/Publications/SPROLLs/world-economic-outlook-database.

Chapter 2

1 Dreher, A. (2006) 'Does globalization affect growth? Evidence from a new index of globalization'. Available at: https://www.iseg.ulisboa.pt/aquila/getFile.do?method=getFile&fileId=503916.

2 President Carlos Salinas de Gortari of Mexico (1993) 'MIT Commencement Address'. Available at: https://infinite.mit.edu/video/president-carlos-salinas-de-gortari-mexico-1993-mit-commencement-address-5281993.

3 Remarks by President Obama and President Peña Nieto of Mexico in joint press conference (2016). Available at: https://obamawhite-house.archives.gov/the-press-office/2016/07/22/remarks-president-obama-and-president-pena-nieto-mexico-joint-press.

4 Frank, A.G. (1998) *Reorient: Global Economy in the Asian Age*, U.C. Berkeley Press.

5 Centre for Climate Change Economics and Policy (2015) 'Seven centuries of European economic growth and decline'. Available at: https://www.lse.ac.uk/granthaminstitute/wp-content/uploads/2015/09/Working-Paper-206-Fouquet-and-Broadberry.pdf.

6 Author's estimates based on Klasing and Milionis, 'Quantifying the evolution of world trade, 1870–1949' (2014) and World Bank data. Available at: http://databank.worldbank.org.

7 Author's calculations using: World Trade Organization (n.d.) World Trade Organization Statistics. Available at: https://stats.wto.org/.

8 Remarks to the World Economic Forum and Question-and-Answer Session in Davos, Switzerland. Available at: https://www.presidency.ucsb.edu/documents/remarks-the-world-economic-forum-and-question-and-answer-session-davos-switzerland.

9 Zoellick, R. (2005) 'Whither China? From membership to responsibility'. Available at: https://www.ncuscr.org/wp-content/uploads/2020/04/migration_Zoellick_remarks_notes06_winter_spring.pdf.

10 Speech on enlargement by Mr Romano Prodi, President of the European Commission. Available at: https://ec.europa.eu/commission/presscorner/detail/en/SPEECH_99_130.

11 Author's calculations using World Bank data. Available at: https://data.worldbank.org/indicator/SH.XPD.GHED.PP.CD?locations=OE-CN.

12 Industrial Federation of Robotics (2023) 'World Robotics 2023 Report: Asia ahead of Europe and the Americas'. Available at: https://ifr.org/ifr-press-releases/news/world-robotics-2023-report-asia-ahead-of-europe-and-the-americas.

13 On China becoming the world's largest exporter, see Federal Reserve Board (2011) *The Growth of Chinese Exports: An Examination of the Detailed Trade Data*. Available at: https://www.federalreserve.gov/econres/ifdp/the-growth-of-chinese-exports-an-examination-of-the-detailed-trade-data.htm. On China becoming the world's largest manufacturer. Author's calculations using World Bank Data. Available at: https://data.worldbank.org/indicator/NV.IND.MANF.CD?locations=CN-US.

14 Author's calculations using IMF data. Available at: https://www.imf.org/en/Publications/WEO/weo-database/2024/April.

15 United Nations, Economic Commission for Latin America, Economic Survey of Latin America 1965, p 8. Available at: https://repositorio.cepal.org/bitstream/handle/11362/1020/ESLA1965_en.pdf.

16 World Bank Group. Available at: https://data.worldbank.org/indicator/TM.TAX.MRCH.WM.AR.ZS?locations=BR-MX.

17 The Global South has become a term used to describe regions in Latin America, Africa, Asia and the Middle East. South – South trade is a term used to describe trade between countries in the Global South.

18 Judt, T. (2010) *Postwar: A History of Europe since 1945*, Vintage, p 581.

19 World Bank Group. Available at: https://data.worldbank.org/indicator/NY.GDP.PCAP.PP.CD?locations=B8.

20 Eurostat. Available at: https://ec.europa.eu/eurostat/databrowser/.

21 United Nations (2002) 'Secretary-General, accepting Moscow award, says strength of Russian spirit "is your country's greatest natural asset"'. Available at: https://press.un.org/en/2002/sgsm8262.doc.htm.

22 Author's calculations using World Bank data. Available at: https://data.worldbank.org/.

23 Congressional Budget Office (2011) 'Trends in the distribution of household income between 1979 and 2007'. Available at: https://www.cbo.gov/publication/42729.

24 Lakner, C. and Milanović, B. (2013) 'Global income distribution: From the fall of the Berlin Wall to the Great Recession', Policy Research Working Paper, No. 6719.

25 Rodrik, D. (n.d.) 'Economics rules: The rights and wrongs of the dismal science'. Available at: https://drodrik.scholar.harvard.edu/publications/economics-rulesthe-rights-and-wrongs-dismal-science.

26 Politico (2016) 'Full transcript: Donald Trump job plan speech'. Available at: https://www.politico.com/story/2016/06/full-transcript-trump-job-plan-speech-224891.

27 Freedom in the World 2024. Available at: https://freedomhouse.org/sites/default/files/2024-02/FIW_2024_DigitalBooklet.pdf.

28 US Department of Defense (2023) 'Military and security developments involving the People's Republic of China 2023'. Available at: https://media.defense.gov/2023/Oct/19/2003323409/-1/-1/1/2023-MILITARY-AND-SECURITY-DEVELOPMENTS-INVOLVING-THE-PEOPLES-REPUBLIC-OF-CHINA.PDF, p V and p 62.

29 LSE Grantham Research Institute (2024) *Strategy and Justice: Managing the Geopolitics of Climate Change*, p 18. Available at: https://www.lse.ac.uk/granthaminstitute/publication/strategy-and-justice-managing-the-geopolitics-of-climate-change/.

30 CSIS (2019) 'Made in China 2025 and the future of American industry'. Available at: https://www.csis.org/analysis/made-china-2025-and-future-american-industry.

Chapter 3

1 Biden, J. (2021) Remarks to the Munich Security Conference. Available at: https://www.securityconference.de/en/munich-security-conference-2021.

2 The Economist (2024) 'China and America trade blame for a world on fire'. Available at: https://www.economist.com/china/2024/05/02/china-and-america-trade-blame-for-a-world-on-fire.

3 Politico (2023) 'Europe must resist pressure to become "America's followers," says Macron'. Available at: https://www.politico.eu/article/emmanuel-macron-china-america-pressure-interview/.

4 U.S. Department of Justice (2022) 'Huawei CFO Wanzhou Meng admits to misleading global financial institution', Justice.gov, 24 September. Available at: https://www.justice.gov/opa/pr/huawei-cfo-wanzhou-meng-admits-misleading-global-financial-institution#:~:text=Meng%20Wanzhou%2C%20CFO%20of%20Huawei,in%20violation%20of%20U.S.%20law.

5 BBC News (2015) 'UK guarantees £2bn nuclear plant deal as China investment announced'. Available at: https://www.bbc.co.uk/news/uk-england-somerset-34306997.

6 European Commission (2024) 'EU trade relations with the United States: Facts, figures and latest developments'. Available at: https://policy.trade.ec.europa.eu/eu-trade-relationships-country-and-region/countries-and-regions/united-states_en.

7 Destatis (2024) 'Order of rank of Germany's trading partners – 2023 (preliminary results)'. Available at: https://www.destatis.de/EN/Themes/Economy/Foreign-Trade/Tables/order-rank-germany-trading-partners.html.

8 Author's calculations using data from Indian Ministry of Commerce and Industry. Available at: https://www.commerce.gov.in/trade-statistics/latest-trade-figures/.

9 BBC News (2020) 'India–China clash: 20 Indian troops killed in Ladakh fighting'. Available at: https://www.bbc.co.uk/news/world-asia-53061476.amp.

10 Data from India's Department for Promotion of Industry and Internal Trade. Available at: https://dpiit.gov.in/publications/fdi-statistics.

11 Author's calculations using United Nations COMTRADE data. Available at: https://comtradeplus.un.org/.

12 Author's calculations using United Nations COMTRADE data. Available at: https://comtradeplus.un.org/.

13 US Energy Information Administration. Available at: https://www.eia.gov/dnav/pet/pet_move_impcus_a2_nus_ep00_im0_mbbl_m.htm.

14 CNN (2021) 'US intel and satellite images show Saudi Arabia is now building its own ballistic missiles with help of China'. Available at: https://www.cnn.com/2021/12/23/politics/saudi-ballistic-missiles-china/index.html.

15 Fulcrum (2024) 'State of Southeast Asia Survey 2024'. Available at: https://fulcrum.sg/tag/state-of-southeast-asia-survey/.

16 The Investor (2024) 'Samsung Vietnam targets 10% export revenue growth with AI-powered phones'. Available at: https://theinvestor.vn/samsung-vietnam-targets-10-export-revenue-growth-with-ai-powered-phones-d8796.html.

17 World Bank Group. Available at: https://www.worldbank.org/en/country/centralafricanrepublic/overview.

18 Energy Institute (2024) *Statistical Review of World Energy*, pp 66–68.

19 All figures are author's calculations using data from the United Nations Population Database and IMF World Economic Outlook Database.

Chapter 4

1 Author's calculations using World Bank data. Available at: https://data.worldbank.org/.

2 Villareeal, M.A., Wong, L. and Grossman, A.B. (2021) 'UMSCA: Motor vehicle provisions and issues', US Congressional Research Service, October. Available at: https://crsreports.congress.gov/product/pdf/IF/IF11387.

3 World Bank Group. Available at: https://data.worldbank.org/indicator/TM.TAX.MRCH.WM.AR.ZS?end=2021&start=2005&view=chart&year=2007.

4 'Factors affecting recent U.S. tariffs on imports from China accessible'. Available at: https://www.federalreserve.gov/econres/notes/feds-notes/factors-affecting-recent-us-tariffs-on-imports-from-china-accessible-20210217.htm#fig1.

5 Blanga-Gubbay, M. and Rubínová, S. (2024) 'Is the global economy fragmenting?' World Trade Organization. Available at: https://www.wto.org/english/res_e/reser_e/ersd202310_e.pdf.

6 IMF World Economic Outlook Database, latest data for 2022. Available at: https://www.imf.org/en/Publications/WEO/weo-database/2024/April.

7 The White House (2021) 'Building resilient supply chains, revitalizing American manufacturing, and fostering broad-based growth'. Available at: https://www.whitehouse.gov/wp-content/uploads/2021/06/100-day-supply-chain-review-report.pdf.

8 European Commission (2021) 'Strategic dependencies and capacities'. Available at: https://commission.europa.eu/document/download/0a5bdf82-400d-4c9c-ad54-51766e508969_en?filename=swd-strategic-dependencies-capacities_en.pdf.

9 Parton, C. (2023) *Chinese Cellular IoT Technology: Understanding and Mitigating the Threat*, OODA Loop.

10 UN COMTRADE. Available at: https://comtradeplus.un.org/.

11 Bounds, A., Hancock, A. and Li, G. (2024) 'EU to hit Chinese electric cars with tariffs of up to 48%', *Financial Times*. Available at: https://www.ft.com/content/0545ed62-c4b9-4e8a-80fa-c9f808e18385.

12 Alicke, K., Barriball, E., Foster, T., Mauhourat, J. and Trautwein, V. (2022) 'Taking the pulse of shifting supply chains', *McKinsey*. Available at: https://www.mckinsey.com/capabilities/operations/our-insights/taking-the-pulse-of-shifting-supply-chains

13 State Council of the People's Republic of China (2017) 'Premier Li calls for stronger China–EU ties'. Available at: https://english.www.gov.cn/premier/news/2017/08/10/content_28147578 1726536.htm.

14 Premier Li on 'Made in China 2025' (2017). Available at: https://english.www.gov.cn/premier/news/2017/08/10/content_281475781726536.htm.

15 Huaxia (2022) 'Xi Jinping stresses mobilizing national resources for core technology breakthroughs in key fields', *Xinhua*. Available at: https://english.news.cn/20220907/9c0e663ad3ee43059a33 f1e57757d53e/c.html?

16 Kynge, J. and Fray, K. (2024) 'China's plan to reshape world trade on its own terms', *Financial Times*. Available at: https://www.ft.com/content/c51622e1-35c6-4ff8-9559-2350bfd2a5c1.

17 The US–China Business Council (2020) 'China in international standards setting'. Available at: https://www.uschina.org/reports/china-international-standards-setting.

18 International Labour Organization. Available at: https://ilostat.ilo.org/data/.

19 Federal Reserve Bank of St Louis (2024) Available at: https://fred.stlouisfed.org/series/MANEMP.

20 Author's calculations using IMF direction of trade statistics. Available at: https://data.imf.org/?sk=9D6028D4-F14A-464C-A2F2-59B2CD424B85.

Chapter 5

1 Author's calculations based on IMF balance of payments and international investment position statistics. Available at: https://data.imf.org/?sk=7a51304b-6426-40c0-83dd-ca473ca1fd52&sid=1542633711584.

2 McKinsey & Company (2016) 'Global payments 2016: Strong fundamentals despite uncertain times'. Available at: https://www.mckinsey.com/~/media/McKinsey/Industries/Financial%20Services/Our%20Insights/A%20mixed%202015%20for%20the%20global%20payments%20industry/Global-Payments-2016.pdf.

3 Bank for International Settlements (2012) Available at: https://www.bis.org/publ/work397.pdf.

4 House of Commons Library (2024) 'Financial services in the UK'. Available at: https://researchbriefings.files.parliament.uk/documents/SN06193/SN06193.pdf.

5 Author's calculations based on IMF balance of payments and international investment position statistics. Available at: https://data.imf.org/?sk=7a51304b-6426-40c0-83dd-ca473ca1fd52&sid=1542633711584.

6 IMF Blog (2022) 'Why the IMF is updating its view on capital flows'. Available at: https://www.imf.org/en/Blogs/Articles/2022/03/30/blog033122-why-the-imf-is-updating-its-view-on-capital-flows.

7 Author's calculations based on IMF balance of payments and international investment position statistics. Available at: https://data.imf.org/regular.aspx?key=60961513.

8 Author's calculations using IMF World Economic Outlook Data. Available at: https://www.imf.org/en/Publications/WEO/weo-database/2024/April.

9 IMF balance of payments and international investment position statistics. Available at: https://data.imf.org/.

10 Author's estimates based on IMF Coordinated Portfolio Investment Survey, IMF Coordinated Direct Investment Survey, and BIS locational banking statistics. Available at: https://data.bis.org/topics/LBS, https://data.imf.org.

11 Author's calculations based on: https://www.morningstar.com/best-investments/china-regional-funds.

12 All estimates by author based on IMF Coordinated Portfolio Investment Survey, IMF Coordinated Direct Investment Survey, and BIS locational banking statistics.

13 BCG (2021) 'Global capital flows in the postpandemic world'. Available at: https://www.bcg.com/publications/2021/global-capital-post-pandemic.

14 Bloomberg. Available at: https://www.bloomberg.com/news/articles/2024-06-26/blackstone-kkr-warburg-invest-big-in-india-private-equity?embedded-checkout=true&sref=hH-Hz8eP1.

15 'U.S. direct investment abroad: Balance of payments and direct investment position data'. Available at: https://www.bea.gov/international/di1usdbal.

16 World Bank Group (2024) *Shifting Shores: FDI Relocations and Political Risk*, p 38.

17 United Nations Conference on Trade and Development (UNCTAD) (2024) *World Investment Report 2024, China Country Factsheet*.

18 World Gold Council (2024) 'China's gold market in May: Gold ETFs continued to attract attention while consumption cooled'. Available at: https://www.gold.org/goldhub/gold-focus/

2024/06/chinas-gold-market-may-gold-etfs-continued-attract-attention-while#:~:text=Currently%2C%20China's%20total%20official%20gold,total%20reserves%2C%20the%20highest%20ever.

19 China State Administration of Foreign Exchange. Available at: https://www.safe.gov.cn/en/2024/0927/2235.html, https://www.safe.gov.cn/en/file/file/20231229/72bf9574b78c4f-1da844ad75d46b0226.pdf?n=Annual%20Report%20of%20the%20State%20Administration%20of%20Foreign%20Exchange%20(2022).

20 International Monetary Fund (2024) *Currency Composition of Foreign Exchange Reserves (COFER), Q2*.

21 Caramichael, J., Gopinath, G. and Liao, G. (2021) 'U.S. dollar currency premium in corporate bonds', IMF Working Paper, p 3. Available at: https://www.elibrary.imf.org/view/journals/001/2021/185/001.2021.issue-185-en.xml?rskey=5egH1T&result=28.

22 Bank for International Settlements (2022) 'Triennial Central Bank Survey of foreign exchange and over-the-counter (OTC) derivatives markets in 2022', Table 1. Available at: https://www.bis.org/statistics/rpfx22.htm.

Chapter 6

1 United Nations (2020) 'International Migrant Stock 2020', Table 3. Available at: https://www.un.org/development/desa/pd/content/international-migrant-stock.

2 Portes, J. (2019) 'The economics of migration'. Available at: https://kclpure.kcl.ac.uk/ws/portalfiles/portal/110383255/Proof_FEA_Economics.pdf.

3 United Nations (2024) *World Population Prospects, 2024*. Available at: https://population.un.org/wpp/.

4 Capital Economics (2022) *The Fracturing of the Global Economy*, p 39.

5 Institute of International Education (2023) *Open Doors Data*. Available at: https://opendoorsdata.org/data/international-students/all-places-of-origin/.

6 Eurostat (2024) 'Imports of oil and petroleum products by partner country'. Available at: https://ec.europa.eu/eurostat/databrowser/view/nrg_ti_oilm/default/table?lang=en.

7 IMF (2024) *World Economic Outlook Database*. Author's calculations. Available at: https://www.imf.org/en/Publications/WEO/weo-database/2024/April.

8 Capital Economics (2022) *The Fracturing of the Global Economy*, p 20.

9 Data retrieved from World Bureau of Metals Statistics (WBMS), 7 September 2024.

10 PIIE (2022) 'Green energy depends on critical minerals. Who controls the supply chains?' Available at: https://www.piie.com/sites/default/files/documents/wp22-12.pdf.

11 European Commission, Critical Raw Materials Act. Available at: https://single-market-economy.ec.europa.eu/sectors/raw-materials/areas-specific-interest/critical-raw-materials/critical-raw-materials-act_en.

12 Bank of England Quarterly Bulletin (1986) Q4, p 513. Available at: https://www.bankofengland.co.uk/-/media/boe/files/quarterly-bulletin/1986/north-sea-oil-and-gas-qb-1986-q4.pdf.

13 Mineral Commodity Summaries (2024) 'Rare earths'. Available at: https://pubs.usgs.gov/periodicals/mcs2024/mcs2024-rare-earths.pdf.

14 OECD Research and Development Statistics, Gross domestic expenditure on R&D by sector of performance and source of funds, 2022, PPP exchange rates. Retrieved 12 September 2024. Available at: https://www.oecd.org/en/data.html.

15 United Nations International Renewable Energy Agency (2023) *Renewable Power Generation Costs in 2023*, p 38. Available at: https://www.irena.org/-/media/Files/IRENA/Agency/Publication/2024/Sep/IRENA_Renewable_power_generation_costs_in_2023.pdf.

16 IISS (2019) 'Australia, Huawei and 5G'. Available at: https://www.iiss.org/publications/strategic-comments/2019/australia-huawei-and-5g/#:~:text=In%202018%2C%20Australia%20became%20the,from%20the%20Chinese%20firm%20Huawei.

Available also at: https://www.theguardian.com/technology/2019/apr/19/where-huawei-is-banned.

17 All figures from IEA (2024) 'Oil 2024: Analysis and forecast to 2030'. Available at: https://iea.blob.core.windows.net/assets/493a4f1b-c0a8-4bfc-be7b-b9c0761a3e5e/Oil2024.pdf.

18 OECD Research and Development Statistics, gross domestic expenditure on R&D by sector of performance and source of funds, 2022, PPP exchange rates. Retrieved 12 September 2024. Available at: https://www.oecd.org/en/data.html.

19 Top Universities 2024, Engineering & Technology Rankings. Available at: https://www.topuniversities.com/university-subject-rankings/engineering-technology?page=1&tab=indicators.

20 Author's calculations using: Nature 2024, Nature Index. Available at: https://www.nature.com/nature-index/.

21 CNBC (2024) 'China's largest chipmaker SMIC is now the No. 3 foundry in the world, Counterpoint says'. Available at: https://www.cnbc.com/2024/05/23/chinas-smic-is-now-worlds-third-largest-chip-foundry-counterpoint.html.

22 The Economist (2024) 'China is quietly reducing its reliance on foreign chip technology'. Available at: https://www.economist.com/business/2024/02/13/china-is-quietly-reducing-its-reliance-on-foreign-chip-technology.

23 Ezell, S. (2024) 'How innovative is China in semiconductors?' ITIF. Available at: https://itif.org/publications/2024/08/19/how-innovative-is-china-in-semiconductors/.

24 IEEE, 2021, More Moore. Available at: https://web.archive.org/web/20220807181530/https://irds.ieee.org/editions/2021/more-moore.

25 See for example CNBC's interview with Intel CEO Pat Gelsinger at the World Economic Forum in Davos, Switzerland, 17 January 2024. Available at: https://www.youtube.com/watch?v=hw-kesm-ktI.

26 Author's calculations using IMF balance of payments and international investment position statistics and IMF Annual Report (2022). Available at: https://data.imf.org/.

27 Niblett, R. (2024) The New Cold War, Atlantic Books – provides an excellent overview of the key issues.

Chapter 7

1 University of Groningen, Penn World Tables. Extracted 26 September 2024. Available at: https://www.rug.nl/ggdc/productivity/.

2 Taiwan Semiconductor Manufacturing Co Ltd (2022), p 8. Available at: https://investor.tsmc.com/english/encrypt/files/encrypt_file/reports/2023-01/84f1ef6f66c6c90b05d2e581066a01a8f1c4f410/TSMC%204Q22%20Transcript.pdf.

3 Canis, B. (2011) 'The motor vehicle supply chain: Effects of the Japanese earthquake and tsunami', US Congressional Research Service report R41831.

4 McKinsey & Company (2020) 'Risk, resilience, and rebalancing in global value chains'. Available at: https://www.mckinsey.com/capabilities/operations/our-insights/risk-resilience-and-rebalancing-in-global-value-chains#/.

5 Chopra, S. and Sodhi, M. (2014) 'Reducing the risk of supply chain disruptions'. Available at: https://sloanreview.mit.edu/article/reducing-the-risk-of-supply-chain-disruptions/.

6 For a summary of the bullish case for AI, Roger Bootle, R. (2019) *The AI Economy: Work, Wealth and Welfare in the Robot Age*, London: John Murray Business.

7 Goldman Sachs (2023) 'Generative AI could raise global GDP by 7%'. Available at: https://www.goldmansachs.com/intelligence/pages/generative-ai-could-raise-global-gdp-by-7-percent.html; Capital Economics (n.d.) 'The economic and market impact of artificial intelligence: How AI will transform the global economy'. Available at: https://www.capitaleconomics.com/key-issues/economic-impact-artificial-intelligence.

8 See for example: PICTET (2023) 'The end of globalization?' Available at: https://www.pictet.com/uk/en/insights/the-end-of-globalisation.

9 International Monetary Fund. Research Dept. (2005) Chapter III *How Has Globalization Affected Inflation?* In *World Economic, Outlook*, April 2006, USA: International Monetary Fund. Available at: https://www.elibrary.imf.org/display/book/9781589065499/ch03.xml.

10 Author's calculations using IMF data. Available at: https://www. imf.org/en/Publications/WEO/weo-database/2024/April.

11 Federal Reserve, 2020, Speech by Jerome H. Powell. Available at: https://www.federalreserve.gov/newsevents/speech/powell 20200827a.htm.

12 Author's calculations using data from China's General Administration of Customs.

13 Author's calculations using Intracen data. Available at: https:// www.intracen.org/resources/data-and-analysis/trade-statistics.

14 Krugman, P. (1994) *The Age of Diminished Expectations*, Cambridge: The MIT Press.

15 Miller, C. (2022) *Chip War*, Simon & Schuster, p 323.

16 Author's calculations using IMF data. Available at: https://www. imf.org/en/Publications/WEO/weo-database/2024/April/.

17 Author's calculations using Penn World Tables. Available at: https://www.rug.nl/ggdc/productivity/pwt/?lang=en.

18 International Monetary Fund (IMF) (2015) IMF Survey: *Sovereign Wealth Funds Must Adapt to New Era of Lower Revenues*. Available at: https://www.imf.org/en/News/Articles/2015/09/28/ 04/53/socar0912a.

19 Davidson, H. (2023) 'Xi Jinping urges China to greater self-reliance amid sanctions and trade tensions', *The Guardian*. Available at: https://www.theguardian.com/world/2023/mar/06/ xi-jinping-urges-china-to-greater-self-reliance-amid-sanctions-and-trade-tensions.

20 United Nations, *World Population Prospects*. Retrieved 26 September 2024. Available at: http://population.un.org/wpp.

21 World Bank Databank. Available at: http://databank.world-bank.org.

Chapter 8

1 International Monetary Fund (2023) 'Fragmentation in global trade: Accounting for commodities'. Available at: https://www. imf.org/en/Publications/WP/Issues/2023/03/24/Fragmentation-in-Global-Trade-Accounting-for-Commodities-531327.

2 UN COMTRADE. Available at: https://comtradeplus.un.org/.

3 Bounds, A. (2024) 'EU prepares two-step trade plan to tackle Donald Trump', *Financial Times*. Available at: https://www.ft.com/content/9b1f982a-485c-4868-9a03-b7e58a6f5746.

4 Congressional Budget Office (2024) 'The demographic outlook: 2024 to 2054'. Available at: https://www.cbo.gov/publication/59899.

5 Pew Research Center (2024) 'What we know about unauthorized immigrants living in the U.S.'. Available at: https://www.pewresearch.org/short-reads/2024/07/22/what-we-know-about-unauthorized-immigrants-living-in-the-us/.

6 There are several reports produced by government and military analysts that provide thorough and regularly updated assessments of China's thinking and capabilities with respect to Taiwan. Two of the most comprehensive are the US Defense Department's annual China Military Power Report and Taiwan's National Defense Report.

7 US Department of Defense (2023) 'Military and security developments involving the People's Republic of China', p 140. Available at: https://media.defense.gov/2023/Oct/19/2003323409/-1/-1/1/2023-MILITARY-AND-SECURITY-DEVELOPMENTS-INVOLVING-THE-PEOPLES-REPUBLIC-OF-CHINA.PDF.

8 The Economist (2023) 'Taiwan's dominance of the chip industry makes it more important'. Available at: https://www.economist.com/special-report/2023/03/06/taiwans-dominance-of-the-chip-industry-makes-it-more-important.

9 SIA (2021) 'State of the U.S. semiconductor industry'. Available at: https://www.semiconductors.org/wp-content/uploads/2021/09/2021-SIA-State-of-the-Industry-Report.pdf.

10 S&P Global Mobility (2023) 'The semiconductor shortage is – mostly – over for the auto industry'. Available at: https://www.spglobal.com/mobility/en/research-analysis/the-semiconductor-shortage-is-mostly-over-for-the-auto-industry.html#:~:text=S%26P%20Global%20Mobility%20estimates%20that,loss%20of%203.5%20million%20units.

11 Welch, J., Leonard, J., Cousin, M., DiPippo, G. and Orlik, T. (2024) 'Xi, Biden and the $10 trillion cost of war over

Taiwan', *Bloomberg*, 9 January. Available at: https://www.bloomberg.com/news/features/2024-01-09/if-china-invades-taiwan-it-would-cost-world-economy-10-trillion.

12 U.S. Department of Defense (2023) 'Military and security developments involving The People's Republic of China', p 141. Available at: https://media.defense.gov/2023/Oct/19/2003323409/-1/-1/1/2023-MILITARY-AND-SECURITY-DEVELOPMENTS-INVOLVING-THE-PEOPLES-REPUBLIC-OF-CHINA.PDF.

Chapter 9

1 Tamma, P. and Foy, H. (2024) 'Mario Draghi calls for €800bn EU investment boost', *Financial Times*. Available at: https://www.ft.com/content/92f7aedd-67fa-488f-8559-7019b7c2e40a.

2 United Nations, 2024. World Population Prospects. Retrieved 26 September 2024. Available at: http://population.un.org/wpp.

3 Author's calculations using IMF data, 2024. WEO data. Measured at PPP exchange rates. Retrieved 26 September 2024. Available at: https://www.imf.org/en/Publications/WEO/weo-database/2024/April.

4 International Energy Agency, 2024. 'Oil 2024: Analysis and forecast to 2030'. Available at: https://iea.blob.core.windows.net/assets/493a4f1b-c0a8-4bfc-be7b-b9c0761a3e5e/Oil2024.pdf.

Acknowledgements

This book is the product of many years of thinking and work with colleagues at Capital Economics. It would not have been possible without them. Foremost among them is Mark Williams, who helped develop the idea of fracturing and refine what it will mean in practice. He is peerless among Asia economists. Julian Evans-Pritchard provided enormous insight into how fracturing will affect China and was a particular help in understanding its tech sector. William Jackson played a critical role in refining my thinking about how fracturing will shape global investment flows. He dealt with my many questions with customary good grace. I am grateful to Vicky Redwood, Andrew Kenningham, David Oxley, Shilan Shah, David Wilder and Jason Tuvey for providing comments on early drafts of the manuscript. They have each improved the book enormously. Likewise, Oliver Wilkes and Hamad Hussain were a huge help in sourcing data.

I am grateful to Roger Bootle for encouraging me to write the book in the first place and for comments on several drafts. Likewise, I am grateful to the Board of Capital Economics, and to Joe Steele, CEO, for their support. I am lucky to work with so many talented colleagues. It is a superb team and a tremendous firm.

Philp Gwyn Jones at Greyhound Literary saw the early potential within the book, and Holly Bennion and her team at John Murray Business were superb at delivering the product. I thank them for the faith they had in me as well as the many revisions they suggested that improved the final text.

Writing a book places an enormous amount of strain on one's family. It requires a huge amount of support and understanding. It also helps when, within that family, you have one of the world's foremost experts on batteries and renewable energy. I'm extremely grateful to my brother, Paul, for helping me understand China's dominance of battery technologies and for helping refine the arguments made in Chapter 6.

Most of all, I am grateful to my wife, Nicky, for her enduring love and support, and children Evie and Josh, for their patience. They have each tolerated hours spent researching, writing and editing when we could have been together. Nicky read several early drafts of the book and persuaded me to keep going when it would have been easier to call time on the project. I'm so grateful that she did and am lucky to have her.

While this book would not have been possible without the help and support of all of these friends, family and colleagues, it goes without saying that any errors and omissions are the responsibility of the author alone.

About the Author

Neil Shearing is Group Chief Economist at Capital Economics, the world's leading provider of independent macroeconomic research and analysis. He is a recognized expert on the global economy and a well-known voice within the investment community.

Neil has written articles in the *Financial Times* and other leading newspapers, as well as appearing regularly on TV and radio, including Bloomberg TV, CNBC, *BBC News* and the *Today* programme on BBC Radio 4. His weekly note is read by thousands of people every Monday.

Prior to becoming Group Chief Economist, Neil was Chief Emerging Markets Economist at Capital Economics, managing a team that won several awards for forecast accuracy.

Neil joined Capital Economics from HM Treasury where he worked as an Economic Adviser for four years in various areas. This included global economics, where he was responsible for briefing the UK Chancellor on developments in China's economy.

He holds degrees in Economics from the University of York and the University of London and is an Associate Fellow in the Global Economy Programme at Chatham House.